Rebecca K

MY KIND OF PEOPLE

Wayne Coolwell, born in Brisbane in 1956, has worked in media-related jobs throughout his career. In 1979-80 he lived and worked in London for a marketing magazine. On returning to Brisbane he worked with an Aboriginal political organisation. In 1984 he began as a trainee with the ABC. He is a broadcaster for ABC television and presenter of *Speaking Out*, ABC Radio's Aboriginal and Torres Strait Islander program. Research on this book has taken him to France, Italy, Thailand, and across Australia.

MY KIND OF PEOPLE

Achievement, Identity and Aboriginality

WAYNE COOLWELL

University of Queensland Press

First published 1993 by University of Queensland Press
Box 42, St Lucia, Queensland 4067 Australia

Typeset by University of Queensland Press
Printed in Australia by McPherson's Printing Group, Victoria

Distributed in the USA and Canada by
International Specialized Book Services, Inc.,
5804 N.E. Hassalo Street, Portland, Oregon 97213-3640

Publication of this title was assisted by the
Australia Council, the Federal Government's arts
funding and advisory body

Sponsored by the Queensland Office of
Arts and Cultural Development

Cataloguing in Publication Data
National Library of Australia

Coolwell, Wayne, 1956-   .
    My kind of people : twleve Aboriginal profiles.

    [1]. Aborigines, Australian — Employment. [2]. Aborigines,
    Australian — Biography. [3]. Aborigines, Australian — Interviews. I.
    Title. (Series: UQP black Australian writers).

331.699915

ISBN 0 7022 2543 6

I would like this book dedicated to a special person who was there for me for the most important years of my life.

Unfortunately I never got the chance to thank her for everything and for making me what I am today, giving me those certain things that you never forget, how to appreciate other people and to love them, regardless of colour, religion or whatever.

She watched over me from the age of five to when she left this earth in 1984.

'Aunty Nancy', I miss you, and I guess words can never express exactly what you meant to me, and to so many others.

But thank you for your love and care. All that I am and all that I do in this life is because of you. You are with me always.

Contents

Preface

Travelling around the world catching up with some of these folks who are living and working in foreign countries was a great lot of fun and a special part of my life which will always be with me. It was a memorable time and included such moments as Big Al at Steamboat Island in Washington State, greeting me with the confused statement: "I thought Aborigines were little pygmies with bones through their nose, who lived in the desert of Australia!"

Then there was the agony of busting my leg after falling out of a coconut tree in Fiji. And having to drive to the airport in that condition after the driver turned up straight from a nightclub and then fell asleep at the wheel. Now that was pretty crazy, with my leg all bandaged up and in a lot of pain trying to make it on time for my flight back to Australia. But those moments, and new friendships were all part of an exciting long journey from the cold winters of America and Europe to the steamy conditions of Thailand.

What a daunting task it was. Just thinking about putting all of this together frightened me a lot, but it was exciting as well. The chance to meet these talented Aborigines, and spend some time with them was a great privilege.

I just want people to understand that Aborigines are different from each other in many ways. We all are bonded by the strength of our heritage, but one person's views about politics and our future role, for example, will vary from another's. And I hope that is what people come to understand about Aborigines after reading about these twelve people. So when you talk about Aborigines, please don't stereotype them. You'll just do yourself an injustice.

I guess more than anything I am more aware of myself now, and how I feel about my country, and how I fit into its future. All of this has made me more contented and more comfortable with being an Aborigine.

I want to thank these people in this book for being who they are, and making me so proud to be an Aborigine. Some have endured such torment, yet they have a wonderful optimism, particularly about the future of their country. I hope people will understand that, as black and white, we live and share many emotions: impassioned, loving and caring — we all want to be happy and not to have to live our life in conflict.

Writing this book was a fantastic journey, something that will always be with me. I can't wait to see the effect these people, and others like them, are going to have on Australia. We all have so much to look forward to.

Artist Gordon Bennett on opening night

Gordon Bennett

ARTIST

There ain't nothing like travelling overseas as far as I'm concerned. Different foods. Different customs. Another language. And strange rituals. I'd been in France many years ago, so I wasn't too worried about having to find my way around. All I had to do was get through customs, get to the main rail system, and just follow the directions Gordon Bennett had set out for me. Sounds easy enough, but what I'd forgotten in my mood of self-confidence was that when I was in France in 1979, I was part of a package tour, where everything was done for you.

The first phase of the operation was a success. I managed to get to the station alright, however from there it became a little more complicated. My destination was Epernay, a small town just about directly east of Paris. What I didn't know was, there was another town with a similar name. This one was spelt Epinay, and was north of Paris.

With the help of Gerry, an Irish fellow tourist, I convinced the lady at the ticket window I wasn't a complete mutant, I was actually asking her for a ticket to Epernay. This was after Gerry had suggested, "Sing it to her ... the French are very expressive, and you have to talk that way for them to understand you." It worked ... only thing was, I was headed for the wrong town.

Gerry and I swapped stories on the train until the seeds of doubt about my directional skills were well and truly sprouting in my head. I was sure Gordon said Epernay was about an hour and a half east of Paris, along the route of the famous champagne district. Gerry didn't know of another Epernay, nor did anyone else I spoke to, or maybe they simply didn't understand me.

This had gone on long enough. My curiosity went beyond an acceptable limit, and a quick phone call to Gordon after getting off at the next stop confirmed my suspicions. We weren't too far out of the metropolitan area of Paris. All I had to do was head for Gare de L'Est station, and from there it was a virtual non-stop trip to one of the most productive wine regions in France. Gerry wasn't in a hurry, so with a bit of time up my sleeve before the train left, we sat down to discuss the last hour or two over a cold beer. After a few laughs, an exchange of business cards, and a personal invitation to visit him in Belfast anytime (surely he was too short to be in the IRA) I was ready to head off.

Gordon Bennett won the Moët and Chandon award for the most outstanding young Australian artist in 1991. His prize was a twelve month residency in France, where he could work if he wanted, and study if he wanted. When I visited him and his wife Leanne in the middle of a European winter, Gordon had been very productive. In six months he had finished five paintings for an exhibition which was going on show in Paris in June, just prior to his return to Australia.

He loved the summer, being able to sit outside and enjoy the countryside, but now with the cold set in, everything looked a bit more dreary. Especially now, surrounded by the skeletal remains of acres and acres of vineyards. We drove up the hill toward his residence at Hautvillers, which means "high village", and Gordon talked about his art.

France has been a reinforcement of the way I've been working.

"France has been a reinforcement of the way I've been working. The language barrier and the feeling of being an outsider in a culture that is very different and a country that is very different from Australia, this relates to my ideas of when the Europeans first came to Australia, and already had preconceptions of landscape and what you do with landscape: you use it as property to make money."

Gordon's little villa was right next to an old abbey, looking towards Epernay a couple of miles away. Out of the tiny collection of cottages on the hill, Gordon had one of the better vantage points. Not even winter could suppress his inspiration. The house was littered with his paintings. In his studio were the latest pieces he was working on. The five for the Paris exhibition were under cover. Here I was, one of the first persons to see exactly what effect this country had on his work, and his inner visions.

The paintings were brilliant. They were full of life, full of anger, yet full of hope. One in particular drew me to it. It was a metre high, a metre and a half in length, in blacks and blues, a three-dimensional depiction of the landing of the First Fleet. Gordon was doing what he really wanted at long last. The search was over. With his art he could finally express himself.

But the journey to this point in his life had been a long one, racked with uncertainty about the most important, fundamental aspect of a person's character ... identity. Like so many before him and after him, Gordon was the victim of a country unable to come to terms with, or deal fairly with, its original inhabitants.

What about the enormous contribution aborigines have made to the pastoral industry, to the armed forces, their sporting prowess, the lives they've saved as black trackers.

It was 1955, and the place was Monto, a small farming community west of Bundaberg. Not too famous, but in the next few years it might just embrace the name of Gordon Bennett, and claim him as its own, albeit his stay there wasn't very long. His father was an Englishman working in the electrical trade, and his mother was an Aborigine from the Cherbourg mission. The family travelled extensively in those early years, ending up in Victoria. It was there during his primary school days, that Gordon got his first taste of what an Aborigine was: *A loin-clothed black fella wandering out in the bush throwing boomerangs and eating witchety grubs.* End of story. Why didn't Gordon jump on the desk and question it? "Mrs Jones, what about the enormous contribution Aborigines have made to the pastoral industry, to the armed forces, their sporting prowess, the lives they've saved as black trackers, what about that Mrs Jones?"

Gordon didn't jump up on the desk, because he simply had no idea he was an Aborigine. He had been starved of the rich and diverse culture which was his right by birth, and he had been conditioned socially as an Anglo-Australian. For various reasons his parents decided that total assimilation was the best path to follow for their first child. They weren't alone of course. All around Australia, the same thing was happening. The philosophy of the authorities was to somehow break the "primitive mould".

Looking back, Gordon holds no animosity towards his parents. His father — the son of a British Army sergeant major in India — had the great British Empire running through his veins. Gordon's mother, deprived of her family and culture, spent most of her early years in an orphanage.

So when the day came when young Gordon Bennett found out he was of Aboriginal descent, well it just wasn't for him. He had been told that Aborigines were untrustworthy and weren't highly regarded. History lessons had taught him that Aborigines were primitive people who wore hardly any clothes and lived somewhere in the middle of Australia. "I really resented hearing that narrow definition because I knew I wasn't like that, my mother wasn't like that." He could see that the only way he was going to make any friends and get ahead in this world was to hide his heritage, to deny it.

I really resented hearing that narrow definition because I knew I wasn't like that, my mother wasn't like that.

Like the old saying, *if you're white you're alright … if you're black then get in the back*, it was a simple choice, but that awakening had a profound effect on his life. The result of all this confusion was low self-esteem, and a lot of frustration. He kept up the charade by denying his Aboriginality, but he couldn't escape the questions like *Who am I?* and *How should I act?* They were repeating over and over in his mind, but damned if he had the answers to any of them. Gordon was even beginning to feel a little uncomfortable in public places. He would find out later the reasons for that. What he did realise was he felt different from other people, and not only because of the colour of his skin. The complexities of all of this would amplify during his working years.

Four years as an apprentice fitter and turner, and then at the age of nineteen, he joined Telecom in Brisbane as a line service-man. Like any young person, Gordon socialised with fellow workers, eager to be accepted into the group. If you didn't go to the pub with the gang, there was obviously something strange going on; you were homosexual, a crawler trying to impress management, or maybe you were just a wimp who couldn't polish off six beers in one hour.

Hey, fellows, have you heard this one? Where does the name boong come from? Give up? Well it's the noise you hear when your four-wheel-drive hits the black bastards! Uncontrollable laughter has them spilling most of their drink onto the floor. A muffled sound comes from the direction of Gordon Bennett. The status quo is maintained, and the boys return to work, satisfied they've got their quota in, and shared a few laughs. All except for one person.

Gordon walked that tightrope in a fine balancing act, making sure he always fell on the right side. He didn't want to jeopardise his job at Telecom, or be outcast. The plan was working. He was accepted and respected by his fellow workers. But those bloody jokes were making him more and more angry, so he didn't join the boys in the pub so often, and started to enjoy his own company a lot more.

All those uncertainties were still with him, and Gordon seemed to be further away from the answers. But maybe, just maybe, they were buried in the pages of psychology books and psychotherapy. On the inside Gordon was screaming out for help. *Why do they ridicule Aborigines for no apparent reason?*

"I felt like an undercover agent in a way. I didn't fit people's stereotypes of what an Aborigine looked like, and so I was privy to their private thoughts about Aboriginal people, and believe me it's not very pretty what they think. I kept it hidden in order to fit in to white society, and to have friends and to get on."

Eventually Gordon found that special something deep inside, the courage to make a decision which would alter his life. With the help of psychotherapy he began to understand himself more,

Gordon Bennett in the garden at Hautvillers, France

and became stronger. He even solved the riddle of his nervousness in certain places: it was agoraphobia. He was diagnosed as having a fear of open places. After eleven years with Telecom, Gordon resigned and enrolled at a Brisbane college for a three year full time course in art. The second most important decision he'd made in his life so far. This time, though, he knew there was much more satisfaction ahead.

He was now thirty years of age, was married, had financial commitments, and certainly no guarantee of even a moderate income through art. But this was his destiny. He felt an amazing sense of freedom, as if at long last the shackles were broken. Now Gordon Bennett was about to make a statement to the world, a statement that had been coming for a long time.

I'm an Aborigine. Whew. I've said it. But it was so difficult to actually say those three words.

"I'm an Aborigine. Whew. I've said it. But it was so difficult to actually say those three words." This most complex of characters who had suffered self-persecution over all those years, sighed. His sigh was heard down the corridors of the past by everyone in the past. He had come home.

There was never any special treatment. Everything he had achieved he had done through his own ability and hard work: the apprenticeship, Telecom. He never asked for anything along the way, and received nothing. Gordon had for a long time been interested in art. He was positive art college would be a wonderful experience, another chapter opening up in his life, and he was right. He earnt high praise from his peers, and created controversy.

"I did a painting which had a devil in it. I had female breasts on it, and I copped a lot of flack from that at the art college because a lot of the arguments were that historically the devil had never been painted with breasts, and you just can't do it. I said to hell with that, I've already done it anyway. And it wasn't an original image, I found the image in a book. It had already been done in the nineteenth century. I had to defend myself over that painting, and yes I did it quite strongly." The challenge was laid down to the hierarchy at the art college, bringing with it a strong message to everyone that if art imitates life, then surely there would be no limitations on one Gordon Bennett. He was awarded straight honours, and the art world admitted someone pretty special, who wasn't scared to be different.

To Gordon there was never any doubt where his inspiration would come from. The powerful images transposed on the canvas were a reflection of the life and times of Gordon Bennett, of the confusion he'd suffered, and still was suffering in this unforgiving world. So strong were the images, after finishing one of his early pieces representing a death in custody, with the words *abo boong* and *coon* blazened across it, Gordon suddenly burst into tears. "The pain in those words, you know, I spent most of my life hiding from these words, I guess." It hurt so much. Now Gordon wanted to use those same words to prise open the conscience of those same people. For them to confront those words, and try and understand the hate they radiated, and to learn from it, and to admit their shortcomings.

He knew what he wanted to do with his paintings. There was no agonising about what would sell the most, or what direction to take, it was a simple uncompromising step, as natural as sunrise and sunset. He had been conditioned into believing some of the lies about Aborigines during those earlier years, and it was about time white Australia understood there was a lot more to these people.

This is the focus of his work, for this Euro-dominated country to consider an alternative to what they've been taught, and especially to what they have heard.

"I want to get people thinking more about Aborigines, to help make them realise those narrow boundaries that we exist in have to be pushed and explored. You know, what we read at school about colonisation and history is only seen through the eyes of a one dimensional viewpoint, from the colonialists. Aborigines didn't see it the same way. And that's what I want to do, change those naive perceptions about history, and to generate healthy discussion. Captain Cook didn't discover this country.

Those so-called primitives wandering around aimlessly

throwing sticks, were intelligent men and women, who had a culture and system working efficiently long before the British arrived." You almost wish Gordon was back in Mrs Jones' class at primary school. Poor lady, I'm sure she would cop a real barrage of rhetoric from Mister Gordon Bennett this time around.

Those so-called primitives wandering around aimlessly throwing sticks, were intelligent men and women, who had a culture and system working efficiently long before the British arrived.

On the one hand he had undeniable brilliance, creating evocative works which were acclaimed around the country, and yet he was still asking the questions and receiving no answers. Identifying as an Aborigine had not taken away the trauma he felt for himself, and his people. He had discovered the cause of the problem, but unfortunately the symptoms still remained. He wasn't alone. A whole generation of Gordon Bennetts were just starting to emerge.

"I feel sometimes like I'm just floating out at sea. Searching and searching for solid ground, for somewhere to land, and to eventually find the peace I'm looking for. I'm just circling and circling, never able to reach out far enough and grab it."

But Gordon wants people to concentrate on his art. He sees himself as uncommunicative, but as for his paintings, they breathe life and energy. And that is what will help people open up their minds, and maybe absorb a whole new meaning. His art transcends time. His paintings, such as the prize-winning *Nine Ricochets: Fall Down Black Fella Jump Up White Fella*, aren't symbolising a historical record of a place or an event in time. They are an alternative, a deconstruction of that blinkered perception of Australia's past, as told by the white storytellers. It is Gordon's cry from the mountaintop about how every Australian's identity is shaped from our history. By deliberately opposing images from that history onto canvas, the painting demonstrates how certain things were left out, and other things were left in, depending on whether you were black or white. Once again it's those narrow borders that must be pushed out for the benefit of not only Aborigines, but for all Australians to reconcile themselves with the past, which is the present, and which will be the future.

My work is about history. How to be Australian through history, and how Aborigines were positioned by that history by our education system.

"The false perception is that the past is separate from the present, and it's not because it all exists in our minds. The past is present and we also have the ability to project what the future will be like, but it's always based on what we learnt in the past, and how we see the present. So that's why I use historical images because the present day Australian identity is based on this notion of the pioneer spirit. But when they recognise that the pioneer spirit was to murder and steal, what does that do to the present perception? It's not divorced at all! People say this happened in the past and you should forget about it, but exactly the same things are happening now. If you don't know about history you are doomed to ever repeat history in the present, so it's not separate. My work is about history. How to be Australian through history, and how Aborigines were positioned by that history by our education system."

Gordon simply wants the truth to be offered up for a change, in place of the romanticism of the white pioneers of Australia, and the myth — depicted in paintings all around the world — of the hard working toilers who all of us can be proud of, for what they unselfishly gave to this country, and the hardships they endured. Gordon takes his hat off to those who did just that, but there are others: for example, those who used Aborigines as virtual slaves on cattle stations. The Aborigines were taken off their own land, and in return were allowed to work for bread, tea, or sugar. When no longer needed these Aborigines were given flour laced with poison, to get rid of them, or rounded up in corrals and shot. Gordon can't comprehend how people still say Aborigines haven't given the country anything. He's tired of those myopic views about Aborigines, and the way these views have dominated the history books.

"I'm trying to put back into the story, those things that were left out, so we have a broader understanding of where Aboriginal people are today. Hopefully Anglo-Australians will then understand our anger and our pain, and when they see an Aboriginal person, realise we have been traumatised by this, and it didn't happen in the past only, it's happening today. Otherwise there wouldn't have been the inquiry into Aboriginal deaths in custody. This trauma still goes on, and we have to live with it daily, and I don't think people understand that."

It's like trying to swim in a race against a white competitor, and you not only have to swim to beat that person, you also have to swim against the current!

For Gordon, nothing has changed from generation to generation. He has so much of that pain inside, you can almost see it.

"It's like trying to swim in a race against a white competitor, and you not only have to swim to beat that person, you also have to swim against the current! And you have to swim with cans being thrown at you, and you have to swim with abuse, not cheering. It's very difficult. How can you ever expect to compete on some sort of equal level?"

Gordon's *Nine Ricochets* won the annual Moët and Chandon prize. He was surprised to win because he expected the judges might be uneasy about putting on the front of their catalogue a painting which is so upfront with its political and racial overtones.

While his work was already in galleries around Australia, undoubtedly the Moët prize would change his life. He knew this was inevitable, and wasn't altogether pleased. As we devoured another french bread stick, Gordon moved uncomfortably in his chair, realising how much more time people would demand of him on his return to Australia. They had already tracked him down in Hautvillers. There would be more to come.

The Moët fellowship was open for all, whatever race, colour, creed or religion. He had succeeded on talent alone, yet bubbling away below the surface was a criticism that he'd achieved all of this on the grounds of positive discrimination ... the colour of his skin had got him first in line ahead of the others. It was those crazy boundaries again.

"I didn't win the Moët prize because I was an Aboriginal artist, which is very gratifying to me because I won it competing as an artist, an Australian person."

On the other hand, some critics seemed to want him to once again deny his Aboriginality. His art was different from most people's idea of Aboriginal art: there were no bark paintings or dot paintings.

"As soon as I'm labelled an Aboriginal artist, people think not only do you have to look like you've come out of a Jacques Cousteau documentary, you have to do dot paintings and roundels out of the desert, or paint on bark. There's a big debate world wide as to the popularity of what is commonly known as Aboriginal art, so I see these boundaries need to be pushed all the time."

He didn't have to live in central Australia and produce that type of art to be an Aboriginal painter. He was married to a non-Aborigine, Leanne Bennett; lived in suburbia; had two cars; two cats; mowed the lawn; and owed the bank money. Yet he identified as an Aborigine.

"I'm in a difficult position where I've been saying I'm not an Aboriginal artist, I'm an artist who's an Aborigine, as a strategy to push those boundaries. What's happening, I find, and this is happening with some other artists who are Aboriginal, is that we're being drawn into saying 'No I'm not an Aboriginal artist, I'm an artist' which is what I've been saying. But it's the same thing as when I grew up denying my Aboriginality, by not identifying myself. It's a dilemma, but at the moment I don't care anymore what they think. They can call me whatever they bloody like, as long as they let me get on with my work."

Sitting inside a warm cottage on a bleak French winter's day, it was obvious that Gordon carried deep scars, the legacy of a country he believes still has a long way to go. His contribution to its ultimate maturity is his art. The critical acclaim and the monetary rewards are secondary to the real purpose, to encourage people to open up their hearts and question present doctrines. He wants to move people with his images.

They don't have one particular meaning, they have many possible meanings. That way a painting lives.

"Sometimes people say, 'What are your paintings about?' Well they're about opening up minds, hopefully. They don't have one particular meaning, they have many possible meanings. That way a painting lives. It doesn't die, like when some people say, 'Oh! this painting means this, this and this.' "

Gordon's paintings moved me in a most vibrant way. I love discovery and learning. Like an event in life that always remains so vivid and true to the end, Gordon's unveiling of his new paintings in France hit me right between the eyes. I'd never taken the time to explore art and the role it plays in society. Those images helped change my attitude. I hadn't felt that aware and in tune with my own spirituality for a long time.

My journey to France had come to an end. Like my previous trip all those years ago, I learnt only a few words in French ... *bonjour, merci,* and *au revoir.* Above all though I'd been privileged to get to know and learn about an artist whose vision and talent would leave an impression on Australia, a country he loved.

"You know success for me is being a more balanced and more whole human being, I think, as opposed to Aborigine or Australian. It's about being a human being, about existing as a person in a country with seventeen million other persons."

Gordon had been both inspirational and manic over the three days of my visit. Getting to know him was a delight. But there were also those moments when he just didn't want to talk to me. It wasn't too bad when we were casually exchanging tales about different things over dinner or checking out the sites of Epernay, but as soon as we talked seriously, Gordon became a little more tense and more aware of his replies. In his quiet tone, he was very careful about what he said. He left me exhilarated, but also very drained. A brilliant man with a magnificent gift, yet at the same time I could see what agony his Aboriginality had caused him, and the scars of the battles.

A train trip through the French countryside would be the perfect tonic for me ... to take a deep breath and place in order the events of the last few days.

As the train left the village of Chalon sur Marne early that Friday morning, my experiences with Gordon had created a most bizarre sensation. His depiction of colonisation on canvas, and the striking images had really stirred me.

I couldn't get those paintings out of my mind. As I looked out the window at the morning mist covering most of the land, that first ever meeting between the British and the Aborigines came to me from out of nowhere. There I was, looking at these foreigners, but through the eyes of one of those Aborigines. My first thought was, who are these people and what do they want in my country. I looked into the stranger's eyes and could see nothing.

It was an extraordinary feeling to have in the French countryside thousands of miles away from home.

I recalled what Gordon had told me: "An artist called Malevich, a Russian avant-garde artist, once said: 'People are always wanting or demanding that art be understandable, but they never demand of themselves understanding.' "

Mark Ella

FOOTBALLER

It was working. I was beginning to come down a little. That drug called Gordon Bennett had sent me on an emotional roller-coaster, but with a little help from some great Australian music — namely Kev Carmody — blaring away on my Walkman, and the soothing effect of a rocking train, I was soon back to some sort of orderly fashion. I wasn't too sure whether that was good or bad though. What I did know was that I had a pretty long train journey in front of me and at the end of the line was a man I had always admired, Mark Ella. Being an absolute lover of this form of travel, I wanted to lose myself wholly in the journey.

My foot was tapping away, and my head was going from side to side, it was fantastic. I knew they were looking at me, but who cares, I've got no shame. I probably wouldn't be back this way again for a while, or maybe never, so, like most people, I made the most of it. The hours ticked away quickly on that first leg to Strausbourg on the German border. While the scenery held my attention for most of that time, it was the final part of the trip into Milan that was breathtaking.

It took about six to seven hours to get there, however the visuals along the way were so stunning that time became irrelevant. I'm sure it is beautiful during the other months of the year, but there's something spellbinding about winding your way down through the Swiss Alps in the depths of winter, completely dwarfed by snow-covered mountains, and surrounded by icy lakes and tiny villages. I hardly moved in all that time, with the music and the scenery complementing each other perfectly. I should have known better though. In my case whenever things are going along smoothly, it usually signals something is about to happen.

That something was the Italian police. At our first stop across the border they entered the train, picking out people at random

Mark Ella, rugby union coach, in the centre of town, Milan, Italy

to search. My mother always told me I looked sweet and inno-cent, and that butter wouldn't melt in my mouth. She obviously hadn't told this particular carabiniere, who spotted me from miles away, and headed straight for me, never shifting his eyes from mine. Most of the passengers were getting the easy treat-ment, a quick look here and there, and *Grazi Grazi*, on your way mate. Well they went through absolutely everything of mine. Being the honest law abiding young man I am, there was nothing to hide, and of course I had nothing illegal on me. They wouldn't be interested in anything of mine … except Oh! No! Not the two bottles of Moët that Gordon and Leanne had given me. For one ghastly moment I thought these two young chaps were going to nick my champagne. Once again my imagination had got the better of me … They gave me a smile and wished me something in Italian.

One memory of Italy that had not faded since my last visit was the traffic: the thousands of Vespas, cars, trucks, and other assorted vehicles that jockey for position on the roads. Well, nothing had changed at all. After learning that Mark Ella was at training, I jumped in a taxi, and headed for the football ground, the Giuriati Campo. It took just three minutes before I was asking for divine intervention. I simply closed my eyes or just stared at the floor for the remainder of the trip. Why put up traffic lights if no one is going to obey them? I didn't dare ask the driver that question, for fear he had an answer.

All I could hear were men screaming in Italian, and all I could see were hazy figures now and again.

They say the fog rolls into Milan as regularly as the vino flows on any night of the week. Well they must have been enjoying themselves this particular evening, because the fog was as thick as pea soup. No matter how hard I squinted, and despite the floodlights on the oval, it was impossible to pick out the figure of Mark Ella. I'd seen him on television innumerable times over many years playing for his country, but on this night my vision was restricted to about five or six metres. All I could hear were men screaming in Italian, and all I could see were hazy figures now and again. Mark must have tuned in to me, because all of a sudden he appeared out of the mist in a track suit and a big overcoat, and introduced himself. Come to think of it, I was the only spectator there, and I didn't really resemble one of the locals.

Mark shook my hand and then shook his head in disbelief at my clothing: T-shirt, jeans and a thin sloppy joe. It was about 2°C and when I thought about it, something *was* wrong here. Mark gave me a big Mediolanum overcoat, but I was actually beginning to enjoy this weather. And if my attire was a little bewildering, the fact these guys were training in this type of weather was ludicrous. The Mediolanum team contained several internationals, including Australia's David Campese, but in that fog I couldn't recognise anyone.

At long last here I was with one of the greatest footballers ever to come out of Australia in any football code — rugby league, rugby union, soccer or Australian Rules — a man whose name is recognised all over the world, and whose deeds on the field gave him legend status, despite his early retirement from the game at the age of twenty-five. But it's not only on the field where Mark Ella gained respect and admiration. His down to earth nature and easy going attitude have won him many friends in many countries. I got an early indication of this when we went for a takeaway pizza later that night at the local hot spot. *Buongiorno!* was the cry from the management and staff at the restaurant, all eager to serve and please this Australian, and all eager to find out about the family, and one member in particular who was their favourite, Mark's five-year-old daughter Nicole. She had a reputation for taking control of everything when she was there. I found this easy to believe ... Aboriginal children have a knack for that sort of thing.

As the coach of the Mediolanum team, Mark was living in Milan. "The Italians in general know where Australia is, they see some Australian shows on television. But not too many people come up and say I look different. I know I'm Aboriginal, the team does, but the average Italian just thinks I'm Australian."

Next day, when Mark's team set out on the seven-hour bus trip to the southern town of L'Aquila, I followed by train. Team policy excluded outsiders from the team bus prior to a match, and Mark stuck to the rules.

It is fair to say that rugby union does not have the highest profile in Italy, although with the 1991 World Cup broadcast live on Italian television, it was generating a lot more interest. I was curious to find out the drawing power of this match, especially with a Mediolanum team full of international stars, including the captain, Campese, Argentinian international Favio Gomez, and about nine or ten Italian national players.

Despite that impressive line up, only about seven hundred people rolled up on Sunday afternoon in L'Aquila to witness their team Scavolini take on the silvertails from the north. The football field was surrounded by concrete stands and steel crush barriers, and fenced off with high wire. I was one of about three or four Mediolanum supporters in the crowd and no way in the world did I feel comfortable enough to openly show my delight when the visitors jumped away to a lead at half time.

Everyone from the program seller up to the coach of the home side had something to say about the score, and the lack of commitment from the players. I didn't have to understand Italian to know their feelings.

In the latter stages of the game, when Scavolini hit back to win 22-16, Mark was unflustered. He gave a shrug of the shoulders, and a shake of the head, and went immediately to his players in the dressing room. He'd suggested to me before the match that it was going to be close. Away games in Italy were known to be twice as tough, for some reason, and although Mediolanum was top of the table, and Scavolini near the bottom, he wasn't totally confident.

His demeanour and co-operation over the next hour and a half was a clear sign of the professionalism of this man. It was fascinating to watch an Aborigine from Sydney, speaking Italian, and handling the Italian media with such aplomb. Here he was outside his team's dressing room surrounded by a dozen or more journalists and photographers, and a horde of officials and fans. Television lights, camera flashes, and a barrage of questions in

Mark Ella's team Mediolanum v. Scavolini at L'Aquila, Italy

Italian. And Mark Ella at the centre of it all. It was another day at the office for Mark, an occurrence that he's become blasé about, but for me it was a very satisfying experience to see him representing himself, his club, Australia, and Aboriginal people, with so much diplomacy.

We are individuals and we should be judged on our ability, not because we were born Aboriginal.

"There are people who think because you're an Aborigine you haven't got much intelligence at all and that really annoys me. I mean, we are individuals and we should be judged on our ability, not because we were born Aboriginal. You've got to project yourself first as an individual and as a person capable of controlling any type of situation. After that, when you've achieved those things on your merits, then you can say, I've done it!"

Mark Ella doesn't pigeon-hole himself as an Australian or as an Aborigine. Undoubtedly he's very proud to be both, especially an Aborigine, but he doesn't wear a banner proclaiming his heritage. His outlook on life is to treat people from all persuasions on the same level, and in turn to be treated, hopefully, with the same respect and dignity. It's a simple philosophy that Mark hasn't consciously engineered. On the contrary, it's a God-given gift that is at the core of his everyday existence. For some of us, communicating with various people in various circumstances can be the most harrowing of experiences, but to Mark it's so natural. He's as comfortable in a pub with some real knock-abouts, as he is at a high society shindig, where he just happens to be the guest speaker. Because of his football career, he's been fortunate enough to rub shoulders with some of the real political and financial movers in Australia and overseas. However, none of that has changed him. If football hadn't come along, he'd still be the same Mark Ella.

The memorable bus trip back to Milan later that night confirmed all of this. His uncomplicated outlook on life, and his genuineness with people make him almost irresistible, to the point where he's become a father confessor to the players, as well as friend and coach. The trip was a lot of fun, the jokes were flying, the beer was flowing, and there was a wonderful camaraderie. To be invited into the private world of a team of international footballers was a real privilege. Here we were, two Australian Aborigines, in the middle of the night, in the middle of Europe on a bus filled with blokes from all over the world, and then one of them puts a movie in the video, and it's *Roger Rabbit* — in Italian. It was the funniest thing I'd ever seen.

Much of my time on the way back was spent considering the amazing contrast between Gordon Bennett and Mark Ella. It so strongly reinforced Gordon's views about the naivety of stereotyping Aborigines. There was obviously a chasm between the backgrounds and personalities of each man, yet they were bonded, by virtue of their Aboriginality. The differences sat me back a little. While Gordon was self-analytical about himself and life, and very self-conscious, Mark on the other hand was candid and very casual. It was interesting to see how growing up in different circumstances had affected them: one had hidden his Aboriginality, the other had no problems with it.

It was pretty hard when you had twelve kids in the family. You're living virtually in a shack, no hot water, no sewerage. I'm probably one of thousands of Aboriginal kids who grew up in the same situation.

Mark was one of twelve children. It certainly wasn't easy for the Ella clan back in those early days on the government-run Aboriginal mission at La Perouse in Sydney. Gordon Ella worked at an oil refinery and in naval stores. He and his wife, May, did the best they could for their children; there was always food on the table, and plenty of good old love and affection. Like so many other large Aboriginal families, which were fairly common back in the fifties and sixties, it was a case of having to make do. They wore hand-me-downs and slept four to a room, but, according to Mark, what they never had they could never miss.

"It was pretty hard when you had twelve kids in the family. You're living virtually in a shack, no hot water, no sewerage. I'm probably one of thousands of Aboriginal kids who grew up in the same situation."

Mark understood the colour of his skin straight away, and was made aware of his heritage and what role he played in it. There was never any clash of cultures at school or anywhere else. It was an easy step from one to the other, from black to white. Mark didn't see it as a divided line: it wasn't the colour of the person's skin, but what was on the inside, which became the determining factor when choosing friends. "We were brought up properly, taught to respect other people. This is the way we are. It's ingrained in us to be this way. All my family's the same."

His personality was already evident, highlighted by his popularity. As for the football, it was there from the start. Not the cold winter days or nights, the pouring rain, the wild westerlies, or the humid summer days could separate Mark Ella from a football.

If only you could open that door to history just a fraction, enough to see hundreds and hundreds of Aboriginal children around Australia playing some sort of sport, all dreaming of being good enough to make the big time, and maybe represent their country one day. For a lot of those naturally gifted youngsters back then, and now, it was the only means of climbing out of poverty, and achieving something.

Mark Ella was one who did, thank goodness. It's almost torture to imagine an Australian rugby team in the early eighties without the brilliance of this man. But history shows that rugby union wasn't the first choice of Mark Ella. He was steeped in the traditions of rugby league from toddler age, continuing to play league on Saturdays for the La Perouse juniors after he entered Matraville High in Sydney with his brothers in the early seventies. The Australian rugby union hierarchy has probably knighted the sportsmaster of that school since then, because the school played rugby, rugby and more rugby. *What the hell! It's not that bad a game … besides, I can fine tune my skills during the week,*

playing for the schoolboys team in preparation for the real stuff
on Saturday mornings.

Mark and the team swept all before them in both codes year after year, easily adapting to the rigorous training and playing schedules. Most times they didn't look the part: they were an ensemble of real misfits, often wearing different coloured jerseys and socks, and always with the appearance of not taking any of it seriously.

Mark was aware that rugby was played mainly by the private schools in Queensland and New South Wales. Aborigines playing the game was a rarity in itself. These factors inspired the Ella boys from Matraville High to produce their best in the selection trials for the Australian Schoolboys rugby team to tour the British Isles in 1976-77. Mark, Gary and Glen each won a place in that young Wallabies team, a side to this day regarded as one of the finest and most talented groups ever to represent this country at junior or senior level. Apart from the Ellas, other players on that historic tour included Wally Lewis, Michael Hawker, Michael O'Connor, Tony Melrose, Tony D'Arcy, and Chris Roche.

On their return, Mark, Gary and Glen joined Randwick, and in 1980 Mark Ella made his debut for his country against New Zealand in Sydney. From then on he became a permanent fixture in the Wallabies team, dictating play and igniting their attacking manoeuvres from his central position at flyhalf.

Undoubtedly for the many purists of the game, the high point of Mark's career was the Grand Slam Wallaby tour of Great Britain in 1984. It couldn't have been scripted better. The Australians won every Test match against the four Home Unions, and Mark became the first Australian to score a try in every one of those Tests. However while the scribes were thinking of new superlatives for this young man, he was about to give them a headline banner: MARK ELLA RETIRES. At the grand old age of twenty-five, and after twenty-five matches for his country, ten of those as captain. No one could believe the news. He was in the prime of his football career, and there was so much more he could contribute to the game. Surely this was some cruel joke! While the rugby world recoiled in a state of shock, Mark gave the final nod.

What the public didn't realise was Mark had already decided, quite some time before, that the 1984 Test against Scotland at Murrayfield was going to be his last match for Australia. He had achieved everything he wanted from the game, and now it was time to put the sometimes unrealistic world of rugby and touring life behind him.

His thoughts were now directed beyond rugby and the life of an international player. He now had to think about his wife, Kim, their family, and about consolidating his future. The well documented upheaval between himself and the Australian coach Alan Jones was very real, but it wasn't the main reason for his decision. It simply helped to reinforce his views that now was the right time to start something else.

But rugby wasn't going to lie down and die that easily. In between promotional work, Mark spent a few years reporting on the game for television and newspapers. Out of the blue he made something of a comeback in 1989 for Randwick, mainly because he was "putting on too much of the beef", and also because Kim was sick of him "hanging around the house". David Campese heard he was back into the action, and invited him to play for his side in Italy. One thing led to another, and before long Mark Ella found himself the coach of the Mediolanum club in 1990.

For the last few seasons he's been spending about nine months of the year in Milan, and the other three months or so catching up with friends and business in Australia. But all of that is about to change forever, and this time he means it. Sixteen years of touring around the world as player and coach, of being away from family and friends, has all been a wonderful experience, but enough is enough. Mark plans to go home for good. Sitting in his two-bedroom flat in an apartment building in Milan, with the snow threatening to fall outside, he envisages the house he wants to build on the northern coast of New South Wales. After being dictated to by so many people for all those years, he's now anxious to use his time the way he wants.

Life for Mark has always been an ever evolving experience, not to be taken too seriously, but to be enjoyed to the fullest, and for him that means the present and the future are the most important. What happened in the past is just memories. For Mark those days are long gone. There are new discoveries for him just around the corner. The way he's glided through the years so far without too many problems, it's almost a foregone conclusion that he'll make the right moves. As for Aboriginal politics being a choice: "It's something I've never really considered before. Straight out of school I worked in promotions and spent ten years doing that. My brothers and sisters are all involved: Roslyn, Gary, Rodney, Jacqueline, Marcia. I guess I've never had the opportunity. I spoke to a few influential people about making my services available. But I never got called, I was never asked. I never got a reply. That was a bit disappointing.

"With my work in promotions, and always being away from my family, and Australia, I've had very little contact with leaders of the Aboriginal community. In some way, I know the problems, but I don't know specifically enough to speak on their behalf. At least those people like Mansell and Foley are trying. I'm not knocking them. At least they're trying, I'm not.

How can you be a proud people if you get everything for nothing?

"Australians in general are lazy, and Aborigines as a people have to fight for our heritage, and we have to be aggressive, and get our backsides off the ground. Australia generally is the welfare country, and Aborigines shouldn't rely on the system so much. We have to encourage the youngsters to get an education. How can you be a proud people if you get everything for nothing?

"Nothing can undo the wrongs committed against Aboriginal people. But if you're worried about what happened all those years ago, we'll never go forward, we won't advance as a race. Aboriginal people need to take the initiative and it's up to them to set their own destiny."

Mark believes that the people at the top of the ladder of government and private enterprise set the rules and agendas. If Aborigines can reach those heights themselves, or if they can influence those people to rethink their strategies, then the domino effect will eventually reach the people who need it most.

Mark has indirectly had a big effect on young Aboriginal people in this country due to his achievements. The role model concept has been an integral part of his life, and something he's been well aware of. However, for some Aborigines, that just hasn't been enough, and it's that sort of talk which Mark has problems accepting: "They begrudge me because I've achieved what they can't. That is not criticism, that's sheer jealousy. What are people like me going to say, 'OK, I'll give all this up ... I'm sorry I attempted to do well for myself, and I'll go back and live on the mission!' Will that make them happy?"

It's the clearest of signs that hidden beneath the persona of this gentle man lies a fighting spirit which won't lie down to be trampled on unfairly. But the handful of critics don't interfere a great deal in his life. While he has major concerns about Australia and its future, his opinions are always kept to himself, or discussed with friends and family. Jumping on the soapbox with a fiery political blurb to force his views down the public's throat has never been his cup of tea. If that's what some people call a weakness, and a cop-out, well they're the ones who have to live with that, because Mark isn't about to defend himself or apologise to anyone.

There's an inner peace that's been with him since the La Perouse days in Sydney which makes him as solid as a rock, and this will be handed down to his two children, Nicole and Simon.

What I never try and do is push a point. I have my own opinions and people can agree or disagree with that.

"What I never try and do is push a point. I have my own opinions and people can agree or disagree with that. It's the same with my children. I hope they turn out to be good human beings, before good Aborigines. By birth they're Aboriginal. I want them to be independent, to make their own decisions."

Driving me to Milan Airport, Mark made a comment which

stayed with me for some time: "I bet I'm the only Aborigine who's been to this city, or even Italy, and worked here." This throwaway line had a great deal of significance. When I had the chance to sit down on the plane and consider what he'd done over the last few seasons, and primarily the example he'd set for Aboriginal people, the remark also scared me, simply because of its raw truth.

I had a sneaking suspicion as my plane headed off to London, that in the great scheme of life, Mark's call-up to Italy would eventually go way beyond a singular accomplishment. Whether he realised it or not, more indigenous Australians would take note and be comforted in the knowledge that they too can set off into the sunset, and succeed, thanks in some small way to Mark's bravado and courage.

Sandra Eades

DOCTOR

Doctor Sandra Eades and I had arranged to meet in a rather swanky little coffee shop on a Saturday morning in the centre of Perth. She ended up at one end of the room waiting for me to come over and introduce myself, while I was right down the other end, hoeing into some toasted sandwiches and coffee, oblivious to her presence.

It's the problem of meeting someone for the first time, and not knowing what they look like. I always feel so embarrassed about going up to people and saying excuse me are you so and so. So I didn't. And I sat there for quite a time before this Aboriginal woman walked towards me, and before she said anything, I knew it was Sandra.

She was casually dressed in jeans and jumper, and was so unassuming and humble, it surprised me. She didn't fit my image of what a doctor should be. I was so glad. Sandra and I got to know each other over a few days, and it was a wonderful time.

Here's her story:

"Take me back ten years, and I would never have dreamed that I'd go to university and study medicine. As a kid I never dreamed that I'd actually become a doctor. It's happened though. It's incredible.

"I had some interest in writing at high school, and I'd also thought of doing a BA, and getting involved in writing. I went to a seminar for year 12 Aboriginal students in Perth. They mentioned that Newcastle University was setting up a new scheme, an entry program for Aboriginal students to do medicine. I didn't think about whether or not I'd get in. I thought, that's what I really want to do. So I just said I was interested, filled in the application forms, went through one interview,

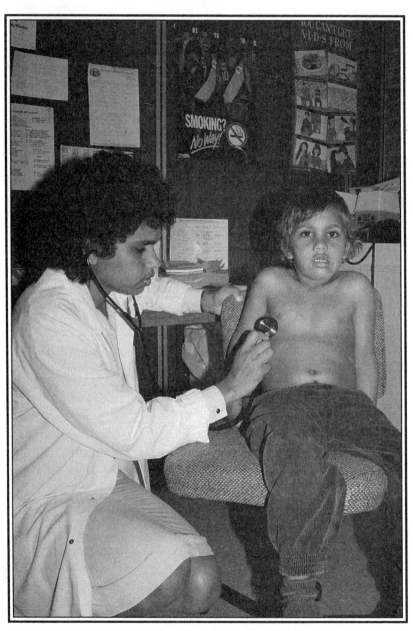

Dr Sandra Eades treating a patient at the Perth Aboriginal Medical Service

strangely enough got through to the next one, strangely enough got through to the week of testing and interviews in Newcastle, and it just came about that I was one of the four people they selected to start medicine in the first year of their program, 1985.

I got the impression right from then that there was something wrong with believing I could actually do medicine.

"I don't know why but my first memory is of being in a class in primary school when I was about nine, and the teacher went around asking all the students in the class what they wanted to be when they grew up. I can remember saying I wanted to be a doctor. The other thing I remember was the real sceptical look the teacher gave me, and his sort of off-the-cuff fling-off remark, "Oh! You'll have to work really hard then." And I got the impression right from then that there was something wrong with believing I could actually do that. In high school I knew that if I had the chance, medicine was what I really wanted to do. But I didn't think it was realistic because I wasn't doing well enough in high school. I thought, I'd like to do that, but I know I'm never going to do that."

"I didn't grow up amongst people who'd been to university. So I had no concept of starting one university course and transferring to another, or starting work and going back as a mature age student. My concept was that if I didn't make it with my marks at the end of year 12, I never would. And circumstances at home, with study, were such that I couldn't see myself building up to be within the top one or two percent in the state, and that's what you needed in Western Australia to get into medicine.

"There was another incident in that primary school class. The teacher was going around asking what all our fathers did, what they worked as. My father had died when I was about five. So when the teacher came to me, I just sat there. I didn't know what to say. And I didn't say anything. There seemed to be this eternal silence. The whole class and the teacher looking at me waiting for me to say what my father worked as. I just couldn't say anything. Some of the kids in the class knew I didn't have a father, and they were looking at me really feeling sorry for me, but not saying anything either. Then the teacher said, "Oh well, if you don't want to tell, that's fine." And he went on to the next person. Those sorts of things don't haunt me, but they're just things that have stayed in my mind.

"Mum worked as a kindy teacher in Mt Barker for about six or eight years. But her kids have been the centre of her life, and we've always known a stability at home. She's been stable, and we've always known her love, and I guess it's built up a good image of ourselves. We've been able to feel good about ourselves. Even now she's always supportive of everything we want to do and she's really proud, but not in an overt way. She's not over the top and doesn't rave about her children.

"It was difficult in our family, with seven kids, and our Mum was a pensioner through most of my high school years. So it was always difficult at home. We had a small house, a three-bedroom house, and I shared a bedroom with my sister. So it was always difficult, and you know as Aborigines your family is so important, you always have a heap of relatives around as well. So it was always difficult to focus. I feel in myself that I did fairly well, because I had to really focus and make it my intention, and my desire to do homework, and to carry on with school. It was there, that desire and that intention.

"But I feel as if I did really well in high school because there were the obstacles of family, the difficulty of finding time to study, of needing to motivate yourself. It wasn't cultural in our family for your mum to be standing there with a big stick pushing you to do your homework, to study, to go to university. It all had to come from within.

"For most of my younger years we grew up in Mt Barker, a small town in the southwest. That was, looking back, a particularly racist town, in the 1970s when I was aged six to twelve. You were looked down upon. You just knew that as a kid growing up. Some of the kids, especially the boys in the class, would always be talking about 'niggers' and 'boongs', and that sort of thing. And I knew that I was one of them. You get a feeling from the way people say things, what it means about you. I once had a friend say 'But you're different to all the rest, there's something not quite right!' But I knew I was like all the rest. I didn't feel that I wasn't.

In Perth there was more an acceptance, and even an admiration of Aboriginal people.

"We moved to Perth when I was twelve years old, and it really struck me this enormous difference between the primary school I went to in Mt Barker, and the primary school I went to in Perth. I guess it helped being a suburb where there were lots of Aboriginal people, but it was really striking. Nobody said 'nigger' or 'boong'. There was more an acceptance, and even an admiration of Aboriginal people, and the same when I went through high school. It was a good thing, a positive thing to be Aboriginal. And by coincidence, one of the boys from my Mt Barker primary school moved to my primary school in Perth. And the only person in the entire school I heard say racist things was this boy who'd switched schools. So it was an incredible difference. I found it much easier to make friends, and lasting friends, like going to my friend's house and sleeping over, all the sorts of things kids do, but which I didn't do at Mt Barker, because I was Aboriginal, I was different.

"I asked my high school English teacher for a reference, and at that point he stopped and he said to me, 'Sandra, you've done really well in English, and I think you have an enormous amount of potential, and I just want to say to you, you can do anything in the world that you want to do. From this point think about it, you're a bright enough individual to do anything in the world that you want to do. If you want to become a doctor, great! I'm going to write this reference and support you in this. But really anything in the world you wanted to do, if you wanted to become a nuclear physicist for example you could.' And I stopped! I stopped and thought, Gee! a nuclear physicist. That was even more incredible than being a doctor.

"My first year at Newcastle University in 1985 was the first year of their program. They add four additional places to their medical school, and for those four places they interviewed Aboriginal students around Australia, both straight from school and mature age. On interview and on testing, and on matriculation results, they selected students to fill those four places, and I was lucky in that year.

"Most medical courses in Australia are six years, but Newcastle and I think one of the universities in Adelaide is still five years.

"The course in Newcastle is different from other medical schools in Australia. They call it self-directed learning, and it's based on the McMaster University in Canada. You don't have pre-clinical years, you don't go for three years without getting into the hospitals, and seeing patients. They combine everything from early on and it's structured differently. The other good thing about Newcastle is that it is smaller than most medical schools, so that in each year there's a maximum of about eighty students. So by the end of five years you get to know the other people in your year fairly well. It's not a lecture based system of learning. You break up into small tutorial based groups. You have about half a day a week of lectures, but most of the other work is in small group tutorials, and self-directed learning ... Going out, studying, looking at your goals, learning things by yourself during the week.

"When I actually went to Newcastle, I didn't realise the enormity of the change. I was seventeen. The only thing on my mind was, I've got the opportunity, I'll go and make the most of it. I didn't think of being away from a family which was so important to me, I packed up and went and did it. A friend of ours knew a few people in Newcastle, and I lived with this family. But I was really focused on making the most of the opportunity. If I didn't make the most of it, it was my failure, it wasn't because the system failed me or because I missed out in any way. So I got there, as it turns out. When you give your best, when you're really focused, and you have a goal, and a really intense desire to succeed and you're willing to work hard and keep your eyes fixed, you just take it one day at a time, and it all works out OK in the end. It was a lot of hard work and sustained pressure for the five years, but I guess I just took it year by year. I really felt the separation from my family, even though in my mind I didn't consciously realise it.

"Every year I'd phone home when I'd passed exams. It would be another milestone and every year I'd get such a buzz. Every year I'd phone home and say, 'I've passed first year' or 'Hey, I've passed second year.'

> **I thought that's a real indictment upon Australia, that Aboriginal people living in an advanced country, have third world health problems.**

"I went to Bangladesh for my third year elective in 1987. It was for eight weeks. A friend of mine and I went to a fairly isolated mission hospital, right up on the northern border of Bangladesh. It was the second poorest country in the world. It had 120 million people in a country the size of Victoria. The striking thing was that, though probably not to the same severity, our Aboriginal health conditions were comparable to third world Bangladesh. I thought that's a real indictment upon Australia, that Aboriginal people living in an advanced country, have third world health problems.

"The hospital was isolated from any of the cities, so it took about two days travel to get there. The operating theatre was fairly primitive. It took a week to prepare the theatre, and then clean it and re-prepare it, so they would operate on the Monday or the Tuesday of every week, treating really extreme cases of everything: TB, leprosy, cholera. For the community health programs we'd get on bicycles and ride through rice fields to get to different villages. It was beautiful countryside. The rice was high, and it was green, field after field of beautiful green rice fields, and it gave you this false image. It looked really pleasant and beautiful, but underneath it all, there was this enormous suffering, and poverty, and kids dying. On our first day, we saw a kid who was just skin on bone, who died of starvation.

As indigenous people it made me realise we're all in the same predicament, to some extent. There's a pattern, and within that pattern there's a unity, because a lot of the struggles we have are the same.

"In Canada I discovered that the Canadian Indians are 'scum' in their own land, in the same way that we are, in a lot of ways, in Australia. The first community I worked in over there was just so encouraging, because they were ten to twenty years ahead of us. I worked with a Mohawk doctor within a reservation. They had a hospital where eighty percent of the staff were Mohawk Indians, and one of the doctors was an Indian. It was like seeing a people in the exact same situation as Aboriginal Australians. As indigenous people it made me realise we're all in the same predicament, to some extent. There's a pattern, and within that pattern there's a unity, because a lot of the struggles we have are the same. I was still a student when I went there. To see that situation was like seeing Australia years down the track.

"I graduated after five years and started working in 1990, my first year as an intern at Royal Newcastle Hospital, then as a resident medical officer at Sir Charles Gardiner Hospital in Perth.

"I don't see myself as someone going out to change the world, but I'd like to make an impact here in Perth, and in the southwest, the places where I grew up. If I make a contribution I'd like to especially put something back into the people around here, and into the system here. Most of what I want to do comes from seeing first hand what that native Mohawk doctor in Canada was able to do within the community he grew up in. I'd like to get involved in general practice, but also researching health problems and formulating how to allocate health resources for Aboriginal people.

"Becoming a doctor is a big achievement. I've realised that

more since I've come back to Perth, and seen the way people want me to join in a lot of the things that are going on. In 1992 I raised the Aboriginal flag during NAIDOC week. That was a big honour. And in 1991, my first year back, I was named Aboriginal of the Year for Western Australia. I'd only just got back in the community, from my point of view, not contributing a lot, but from the point of view of the Aboriginal community, just doing what I'd done and coming back, and identifying, and being involved in the community, was a positive thing.

"I get the feeling that people would like to enlist me and that I would be a good frontline person for a cause. I've been involved with my job in the public hospital so I haven't been on the street, I haven't been working in Aboriginal organisations. I haven't been rubbing shoulders and getting a good feel for the issues. I've been involved with the Aboriginal Advancement Council, supporting and getting that going in Perth again. There are people out on the street getting a better feel for all the issues, who are better spokespersons, and yet I get asked for my opinions.

"I feel as if Aboriginal people have achieved a lot already. I have a fairly positive view, not so much about what the government can do, or the reconciliation council can do, but more for what we can do for ourselves. Just within my own family, and my own contacts, I think we've gone an enormous way already within the period of one generation. My grandparents didn't get the chance to go to school, my parents certainly didn't get the chance to go to high school, and yet within that one generation or so I've had the chance, to finish all my schooling and go through to university, and achieve something that way. There's an enormous number of changes we've gone through since 1967 when we were formally recognised as people, as citizens in Australia. And to come to the stage where, from all that oppression, within such a short period of time, we have a number of people graduating as doctors, and lawyers, pushing out into the community, that really encourages me. I see it as an emerging change. A lot of people would say that it's too slow, that it's appalling that there are only seven or so Aboriginal doctors in Australia, but I see it as fairly positive.

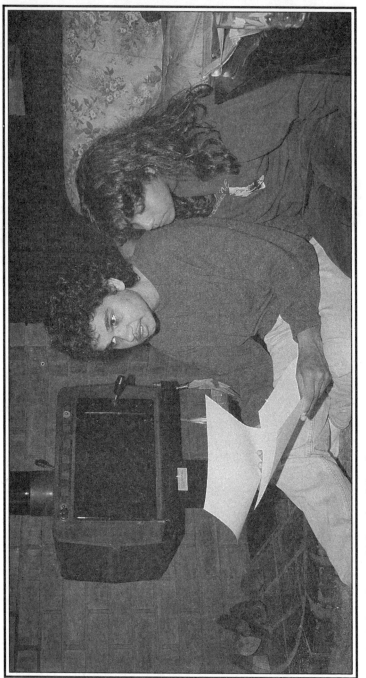

Sandra Eades at home with her niece Miranda

"I don't think people realise the enormous number of Aborigines, compared to five years ago, coming through tertiary institutions. I get a real buzz talking to my nieces and nephews. As someone they see day in day out, who's achieved something, who's not the stereotype of an Aborigine, I tell them they can change their image of themselves, feel good about themselves, realise they're as valuable and gifted as any other member in Australia. We're emerging. We're a people taking control of our destiny.

"When I was younger, I used to feel really unsure and maybe in some ways a bit embarrassed about being Aboriginal. But as I grew up, and as one experience added up on top of the other, and as I thought about what our family and what our whole culture and all our people mean, being Aboriginal and being a Nyungar was something to be intensely proud of, something I'd always wanted to identify as. Comments like 'Oh! But you're not like the rest' are actually an insult.

They think that by suggesting that I'm part-Aboriginal, or that I've had white ancestors, that it's a compliment.

"Some people see me as an exception, as not really being an Aboriginal. They think that I must have some other heritage, that I'm not totally Aboriginal, and maybe it's the white part. But my parents and my grandparents are all Aboriginal. Some people try to explain away what I've achieved by speculating what white heritage I must have. And that is a bit disappointing. They think that by suggesting that I'm part-Aboriginal, or that I've had white ancestors, that it's a compliment or that I'm above and better than any other Aboriginal person. But I am an Aboriginal, a Nyungar from Perth in the southwest. It's something to be really proud of, because I see us as a people with a tremendous heritage and a tremendous sense of family, and a lot of values that are really important.

"It's a really powerful thing for someone to come to hospital and have as one of their primary carers, one of their doctors, an

Aboriginal person. It just challenges all their beliefs, everything they've expected of Aboriginal people all their life. Because there's an enormous amount of respect for doctors, it's like they come to this point where there's a big clash of both views. I've been asked whether I've encountered racism at work. What happens is that people see me as a doctor first and foremost, and then Aboriginal. If anything, it's been a really positive thing. People tend to stop and congratulate you, and say how well you're doing, and start talking about someone they knew years ago, and what contact they've had with Aboriginal people, if any.

"I know that when I go to work I'm making a statement for Aboriginal people, and so far it's been good. I know that what I'm doing at work is a positive thing. I haven't found it a burden. In fact it's more like a privilege. It's a strange thing, but just by being at work, just by being in your situation, you're a positive role model in your work place for Aboriginal people. The unfortunate thing is that most people tend to hold on to their ignorance and their racism. They tend to see you as an exception rather than change their actual beliefs about Aboriginal people. But there are a lot of people who are open to change.

"It's the whole thing about changing people's perceptions, making them realise how incredibly talented and full of ability Aboriginal people are, and, given the opportunities, how well we do.

"Probably one of the most touching things that has happened to me was when I worked in geriatrics in 1991. There was a gentleman who was about ninety years old. He'd spent all those years in Australia, and he'd worked on a farm, and he'd also worked in the city, and he'd had Aborigines back in the fifties and sixties working on his farm. For him to see an Aboriginal working as a doctor, to have achieved something ... he just congratulated me. From his point of view, Australia was changing, and opportunities and breakthroughs were finally being made.

"One of the biggest pleasures of my job is being able to make Aboriginal people comfortable in a place where they feel so uncomfortable. Recently we had a lady from the northwest on our ward, and she was just so shy, and you could just feel that she felt she was in another world. To be able to sit down and talk to her, and say 'Oh! Where are you from? Who are your people?' to ask her about her kids and how they must miss her, it helped her so much.

"Actually one of the other doctors overheard me talking on the phone to an Aboriginal person. The doctor said, 'You change when you talk to an Aboriginal person on the phone. It's like you make a connection.' "

Sandra Eades fulfilled her dream of working with her people and is now on permanent staff at the Perth Aboriginal Medical Service.

Where land rights advocate Noel Pearson is often found … behind a microphone

Noel Pearson

LAND RIGHTS ADVOCATE

I first met Noel Pearson in Brisbane in 1991. The Queensland Labor government had just passed its controversial Aboriginal and Islander Land Act. There was a backlash around Queensland by some Aboriginal groups, who vented their anger with marches down city streets. In Brisbane there was a confrontation with the police outside the gates of Parliament House, which led to some arrests. Noel Pearson was giving media interviews, highlighting what he saw as the problems with the legislation. When we spoke that day he never took his eyes off mine.

Noel Pearson is unrelenting. When his people at the Hopevale Aboriginal Community in North Queensland wanted to improve terms for sand mining on their land, Noel was at the centre of negotiations as a representative of the Cape York Land Council. The council ignored the usual procedures of going to the state government, and instead went directly to the Japanese-owned mining company, and got a better deal for Hopevale.

No decision was made without the knowledge and consent of the rest of the community, but the state government was by-passed altogether. The whole deal was struck between the executives of the company and the land council without government officials sitting in or determining the outcome.

The Cape Flattery Silica mining company had been sand mining on the traditional lands at Hopevale for a quarter of a century, paying a small royalty from the profits back to the community. When the time came to renew the mining lease, both parties sat down, and after a bit of pushing and shoving, they reached an agreement. The new contract negotiated by Noel and the land council has now given Hopevale a substantially bigger share of those profits, around a million dollars annually, as well as more jobs for the community. But more importantly, it has given economic strength for the future.

Had the community accepted the usual legislative arrangements for benefit payments, they would have ended up with a much smaller amount to work with at the end of the day. Under the new arrangement they now have well in excess of the original royalties, and provisions such as employment, training, conservation of the area, and hunting and fishing access to some areas.

That's just the start of it. Noel has a dream of what this new economic stability will lead to. The Hopevale people are on the threshold of something very exciting. They can now purchase enterprises, such as small businesses and farms, to establish a strong political and business base. No more will most of the money be lost into white pockets. This gives the community the chance to compete on an equal footing, with money which is controlled by the Guugu Yimithirr entrepreneurs, not the government.

I came to realise that Noel, a history honours graduate and law student, wasn't prone to making loose statements. Everything was calculated when he discussed issues like this. There's an infectious energy surrounding him when he talks about Cape York. Noel and the council won't stop pursuing their dream for this magnificent wilderness ... this is his country, and he'll fight for it. The benefits are there not only for the Aborigines, but for non-Aborigines. You can't mistake the conviction when he says, "This beauty must not be lost by Aboriginal people."

Noel believes Cape York is the last great traditional domain left in Australia for Aboriginal people. It should be put in the same category as the Great Central Desert, the Kimberleys, and Arnhem Land. All those areas have long been recognised as Aboriginal land, and treated as such. The Queensland government has secured some regions of the cape by declaring it national park, but for Noel and the council it is still not in the hands of its original owners.

Ever since he was a child, Cape York and the land has been his inspiration ... he cannot see it any other way.

"It would be difficult for most Aboriginal people to pursue a career or do things that are not somehow involved with their people; with their people's political struggle."

Aboriginal politics is Noel Pearson's life, but the talk of

sovereignty or establishing self-government for Aboriginal people makes him pause. You see, ideologically he believes in it, but the worry is that the short term objective of land rights for Aborigines will become that much harder to sell as a proposition to the government if the emphasis is placed on the sovereignty debate. He sees land rights as an issue that has been pushed into the background by the past federal governments.

> **In this country land rights is just seen as: put a bit of real estate under Aboriginal feet to quieten them up.**

"Countries like New Zealand and Canada have long talked about the need for settlement rights, whereas in this country land rights is just seen as: put a bit of real estate under Aboriginal feet to quieten them down. In the USA, Canada and New Zealand, land rights has meant a full and proper settlement, not just real estate. It's compensation, it's empowerment for economic development, so it's really more than anything a national constitution.

"The indigenous people of Canada had original sovereignty over their land. The new white sovereignty has usurped those original rights, and therefore there is a need to reach a settlement with the indigenous Canadians in recognition of that usurpation. The same thing has to happen in Australia.

"Land rights across this country has basically been restricted to vacant crown land and available public land, rather than private lands held by other Australians. But what's got to be recognised is that Aboriginal people have been left with the remnants. Aboriginal reserves were created across the country, scrap lands that were set aside for 100–150 years ago. Many were subsequently revoked and given to white people. Most of the Aboriginal reserves in New South Wales were revoked after World War I and II, to give to returned soldiers."

Noel believes that until the Commonwealth assumes direct responsibility for Aboriginal people by reaching a final land rights agreement, there will be no proper and just compensation for Aborigines. He's tired of the inconsistencies of the different states and territories.

"Tasmania has nothing. Victoria has basically two reserves. New South Wales has funding of land rights from land tax, but a very small amount of land is held by Aboriginal people. South Australia has very good provisions for traditional groups in the north, but nothing for town dwellers in the south.

"The Commonwealth has given rights to traditional groups in the Northern Territory, but nothing to people who have been dispossessed by cattle stations and are living in towns.

"In Western Australia some land is under some form of Aboriginal control, but the nature of the title, and the control they have is very poor compared with the Northern Territory.

"And of course in Queensland there is no provision for town-dwelling Aboriginal people, and minimal provision for traditional land claims."

Don't lose the faith just yet though. The High Court Mabo verdict in 1992 may change some things. On one side you had Eddie Mabo and some people from Murray Island in the Torres Strait refusing a deed of grant in trust title by the Queensland government to their land. They based this on the premise they were the original occupants, and therefore nothing had changed. They didn't need an official piece of paper from the state government suggesting otherwise, when they already owned the land.

In the other corner you had the government promulgating the crown law and the enactments which over the years had extinguished any legitimate claim by the islanders. It was a classic contest of common law versus the crown.

Those judges sitting in the High Court of Australia found in favour of the late Eddie Mabo, handing down a judgment that native title to land did exist. The decision virtually dispelled the myth of *terra nullius* (empty land), where the British claimed Australia as theirs on the basis that it was uninhabited before they arrived. For Noel and other Aborigines around Australia those judges have now been feted as having finally brought Australian law to the same position of justice reached by the United States Supreme Court in the 1820's. Finally, Aboriginal politics will be elevated to stark reality instead of the fairytale dimension some people regard it as, all because of this historic verdict.

"I heard a Native American talking at a Mabo conference, and he said, 'Prior to Mabo you people had nothing! In terms of your position at the bargaining table you had nothing, whereas now you have a great bargaining tool.' And it's a fact. All we had was a moral claim against non-Aboriginal people and governments. We didn't have a legal and a moral claim which we could enforce. My own personal fear though is that without resources we're going to see native title eroded right across the country. Remote Aboriginal groups without resources to go to court, to assert their native title right, won't be able to stop extinguishment where it is threatened. Without resources those groups are going to get rolled all the time.

"Unless there is some kind of remedial legislation put in by the commonwealth or the state to protect from further extinguishment, I feel pessimistic about the prospects of saving native title across the country.

I mean two of the most robust mining and industrial countries on this planet, Canada and the United States, are two jurisdictions in which 'native title' has been an accepted fact for a long time.

"I mean, two of the most robust mining and industrial countries on this planet, Canada and the United States, are two jurisdictions in which 'native title' has been an accepted fact for a long time. And no attempt has been made to qualify it or extinguish it."

The one thing Noel has learnt since immersing himself in Aboriginal politics, is that his people don't know how the media works, and how to use it to their advantage.

It is an unfortunate irony that Aboriginal flags and marching in the streets can be vote winners for the politicians who are hailed as heroes when they confront them or simply ignore them.

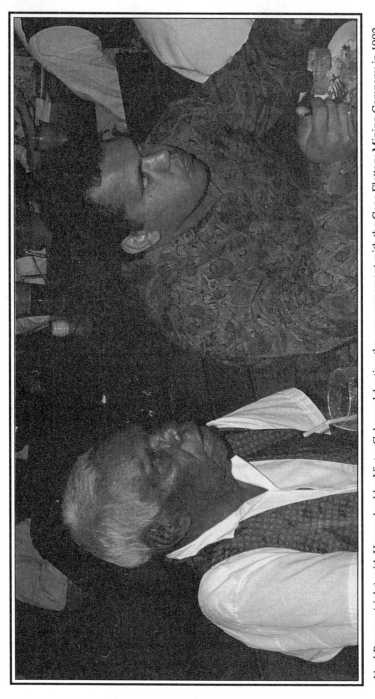

Noel Pearson (right) with Hopevale elder Victor Cobus celebrating the new agreement with the Cape Flattery Mining Company in 1992

Bjelke-Petersen lost no votes when he confronted Aboriginal protestors.

"Basically the Aboriginal cause has about a third of the Australian population under its belt, in support of some measure of land rights. To capture the hearts and minds of more people might involve an education and awareness program. But it must have specific aims, and not just make people warm about Aborigines.

It's no good making people feel good about Aboriginal art, and Aboriginal culture, and making people feel that Aborigines are cuddly bears.

"It's no good making people feel good about Aboriginal art, and Aboriginal culture, and making people feel that Aborigines are cuddly bears. No one will benefit from feelgood messages without real change being made to the position of Aboriginal people in this country."

Noel has been approached to take that next step into party politics, but, steady on, the thought of consorting with the enemy at this stage of his life doesn't make a whole lot of sense.

His first brush with politics was not a happy one: as the representative of the Cape York Land Council, Noel was invited by the Queensland Labor government to sit on the cabinet committee to draft the Aboriginal and Islander Land Acts Bill of 1991. He became extremely disenchanted with the process, and lack of commitment from the government side. He resigned in protest. His fears became reality, and the eventual Act did not please Aboriginal groups.

There were a couple of things Noel was angry about. Provisions he thought were going to be in this new legislation were completely overlooked. What also angered him was the deceit of some of the politicians, who, according to Noel, had promised their support with a handshake, but when the time came to stand up and be counted, they had done an about-face.

One of the big criticisms Noel had with the Land Act was the failure to provide an acquisition land fund for Aborigines. Under the legislation only vacant crown land and national parks are claimable, therefore a big percentage of the indigenous people in Queensland who don't have access to these particular lands get nothing.

New South Wales has a fund set up addressing that issue, where a certain percentage of land tax revenues from the state goes toward that fund. Noel is worried that Aborigines in urban areas, for example, cannot claim lost traditional lands or receive reparation for that loss."

It is still possible for mining companies to mine on Aboriginal land notwithstanding the objections of the Aboriginal land owners.

The Queensland Labor government's legislation on mining was no better than the National Party's. According to Noel: "It is still possible for mining companies to mine on Aboriginal land notwithstanding the objections of the Aboriginal land owners."

This setback taught Noel many lessons. It was a personal disappointment after all the lobbying the Land Council had done. But Noel puts it in perspective by observing that the old traditional owners in Cape York had been struggling from before he was born, they had suffered disappointment more often than not, and they were still struggling. Noel and the Land Council continue to fight for the traditional people of far north Queensland with the same fervour.

Noel's path to the world of politics could be seen as a natural development for an enthusiastic and articulate young person who wanted to do something for his people. One thing leads to another.

Unlike most other Queensland reserves Hopevale and another, Wujal Wujal, were overseen by the Lutheran Church. The board of governors sent certain Aboriginal children to church boarding schools in Brisbane. In 1978 Noel left the small fibro house where he and his siblings had been raised and went to St Peter's College in Brisbane.

If he was one of the king pins at primary school up north, he was very quickly demoted to insignificance in this new regime at boarding school. Initially Noel found it rather daunting, and the adjustment took some time. Science and maths had been on the periphery at Hopevale, but they commanded a higher profile at St Peter's, and caused the biggest headaches.

With excellent results in English and History, Noel enrolled in an arts degree at Sydney University. He didn't quite stretch himself over those four years, though he graduated with honours. His honours thesis was on the history of Hopevale, and what he learnt brought him closer to his people.

His research helped Noel fill in the pieces of his own history. It was just what he was looking for, and set him on the road to more study, this time in law. He saw that law offered a very powerful leverage for debate and hopefully eventual change. Noel desperately wanted a chance at both.

He deferred university and got back to his family and friends at Cape York. This is when it all started for Noel Pearson. He was elected to the Aboriginal Community Council in 1988 and 1989.

This experience prepared him for the next few years, fighting for the future of Cape York and its Aborigines. It's what he does best. Give him the audience, and simply let the rest take care of itself. Whether he's on the phone in the land council office in Cairns talking in the Guugu Yimithirr language to one of his people, or before state political and community leaders in full flight condemning the total frustration of the land rights process, Noel Pearson always leaves them thinking.

Wayne Costelloe: overlooking the beautiful Phuket coastline, Thailand

Wayne Costelloe

AUSTRALIAN VOLUNTEER ABROAD

There's an annual tribute to the teachers in Thailand, that typifies their value. Representatives from each class present flowers of appreciation to the teachers. When Wayne Costelloe, an Aborigine from Rockhampton, began teaching on the island of Phuket, he found this ceremony extraordinary.

He sat on a stage while one of his pupils walked toward him. When she reached a certain point, with the flowers still clutched in her hand, she crawled across the stage. She presented the gift to Wayne and retreated backwards in exactly the same fashion, her head bowed all the time. What an initiation for this Aborigine from North Queensland. He'd certainly never seen anything like that before.

I spent a few days in Phuket at the teachers college where Wayne Costelloe was teaching English. What an eventful four days that was. I arrived only a few weeks after the May 1992 upheaval between the pro-democracy students and the army in Bangkok, where it turned into a battlefield with the students coming off second best. I could feel the aftermath still lingering. Some of the students and teachers at Wayne's college, The Rajabhat Phuket, had demonstrated against the army. Many were still willing to talk about it, vehemently denigrating the system for creating such a mess in the first place.

The institute was on about five hectares. There were another thirty-five of these colleges on the mainland. All up at Phuket there were about 1,000 regular students, and 2,000 in-service students who were fulltime students attending lectures on Saturday and Sunday. There were six faculty buildings, and it was obvious that not too much money had been spent on this institute. I turned up unannounced, so it took a while to find Wayne Costelloe. Now if I had asked to see Ajarn (teacher) Waykin, the

Australian Volunteer Abroad, then no worries, but what's life without a bit of confusion.

Teachers are treated as pure gold, and respected as such, in Thailand.

Teachers are treated as pure gold, and respected as such, in Thailand. In the class structure they are right up there, much higher than lawyers, for example, who are looked upon with a fair bit of scepticism. I was on an official visit, so I had it made in the shade. Like some sort of high ranking dignitary, I was introduced to this person and that, and most of the time did not really have too much of an idea what the heck was going on. I'm not comfortable with people bowing to me, treating me as if I'm more important than they are. I felt I wasn't giving them anything in return for their hospitality. I was the visitor in their country, however, and I had to respect their customs, which meant I could not complain. That would disgrace them.

But surely it's not right to drive past poverty, and act like it doesn't exist. A lot of these Thais will never know anything else, or even take a step outside the boundaries they're enclosed in. They will never, never have any opportunities in their life to rise above that. So much sadness for me, but not for them. They are just beautiful people. They love life, and when they smile at you, their whole face tells the story.

Wayne had discovered something eerie. Some of the ethnic Thai, and the Chinese Thai, had a strong resemblance to Aborigines back home. I noticed it too. It wasn't so much a physical but a personality likeness: an occasional gesture or mannerism. Just as Aborigines will almost always wait for the other person to go first, the Thai teenagers I met at the institute did exactly the same.

"Like Murris at a dance, hey?" Wayne said to me on my first day. "No one will dance until the lights are turned off. It's the same here. When that light goes off, everyone scatters. The ethnic Thai are the darker skinned people, and they're the indigenous people of this land. They have a sharing and caring similar to what we have in Aboriginal culture." Was there some connection from the past? Perhaps it dated back to a cultural unity found in the history of the Asian region when the countries were a single mass eons ago. All of this was a healthy coincidence for Wayne, who enjoyed the likeness, as it made him feel a little more at home.

Wayne Costelloe was born in 1965 in Charters Towers, Central Queensland, and went to Catholic schools including St Brendan's Christian Brothers College in Yeppoon. After completing his Bachelor of Education at James Cook University in Townsville, he worked as a government education officer with Aboriginal programs including ABSTUDY, a scheme to give financial assistance to Aboriginal and Islander tertiary students. For a time he was a programs officer with the Aboriginal Arts Unit of the Australia Council in Sydney. While in Sydney he joined Australian Volunteers Abroad.

To find out how Wayne Costelloe came to this point in his life, roll back the calendar to his final year at St Brendan's when an event influenced him greatly. "I had a teacher who loved my writing. He absolutely loved it. He always used to stand me up in the class and say, listen to what Wayne Costelloe wrote. This particular time I had to write this essay for a test, and he said, 'Wayne, you should be a diplomat, this is wonderful'." Wayne never forgot those words. A year or so later, he went right to the source, and was invited to sit for an initial test for the Foreign Affairs department, followed by an interview. That's where he came to a screaming halt. He didn't make it to the next stage, and he suddenly realised how difficult achieving his ambition was going to be. Not impossible, though.

Becoming an Australian Volunteer Abroad was a part of the journey, and it all made sense ... instinct was leading the way, so why not throw yourself at its mercy, and see what happens. Why deny the impulses? From way back, he knew the world overseas would one day call him, and not simply as a tourist, but to make a worthy contribution to another society, to help those who really needed it.

On the plane to Thailand Wayne realised it was too late to turn back. "I was so nervous and shaking badly, thinking I'm actually on this flight heading to a different country I hardly know anything about. What are they going to be like? Do they know anything at all about Aborigines?" As well as his own fears, he carried the doubts of others back home. "People would say to me, why go overseas when you should be having a look at your own backyard? I said, why not? I still see myself contributing indirectly to the Aboriginal people by being overseas. Hopefully I'll be able to change the stereotypes by advancing myself."

What are they going to be like? Do they know anything at all about Aborigines?

His first impressions of Thailand were not complimentary. The first few days of pollution, noise, and poverty, were frightening realities of a country far removed from the comparable bliss of Australia. Some of the Aboriginal communities he had visited back home were akin to third world conditions, but Wayne had not seen such utter misery as some of the sights he saw on the streets of Bangkok. Some of these people were completely lost souls, and a lot of them children. As the weeks passed, he became more resolute about the situation, and the awkwardness was replaced by a more disciplined approach to his adopted country. He never did like Bangkok, but had to suffer quietly, because he had no choice. As an Australian Volunteer Abroad, Wayne had to spend his first few months in the capital.

Phuket island was all hustle and bustle. With a population of 167,000, it is one of the biggest tourist centres in Thailand. Wayne's students were curious: was he an Indian? An Afro-American? Or maybe a Pacific Islander? Everything but his own race. Wayne had a lot of fun teaching these students about the indigenous people of Australia, and a real bond began to develop between teacher and students.

Only a few hours after arriving in the country, I got a pretty good idea of how much Wayne had fitted into his new surroundings. We were heading into town for a coffee and a get together with Wayne's French class. He was studying French a couple of nights a week. I had a niggling sense of insecurity about this, but if Wayne felt easy, then it must be alright. The next fifteen minutes was a nightmare. Here I was on the back of this little step-through motorcycle, without a helmet, clinging on for just one more day of my life, darting in and out of the cars and what seemed like thousands of other motorcycles. They were just mad! It was like I was in the middle of some B-grade bikie movie, with all these loonies ripping around without any regard for road rules, and all with some false illusion of immortality. You haven't seen anything until you've seen four generations of a Thai family, in shirts, sarongs and sandals, squeezed onto a step-through ... grandma second from the front, with the great-granddaughter almost obscured, right behind her ... and no helmets, any of them! Wayne had now become one of them, without any problems. He was good, and we got there without any mishaps, but it was the first and last time I jumped on one of those things. The next day I hired a car.

Funny how you slowly transform when sheer chaos envelops you. A few months earlier I was reciting Hail Marys in the back of an Italian taxi, and before that I was rebuking the French rail system for getting me lost. And now here I was in Phuket and I was ashamed of myself: my driving habits and road courtesy disappeared out the window. After a few days I was beeping the horn at anything that moved, and charging around like those roads were mine. I don't know what it was, but I just got caught up with the tempo of life. It'll do it to you every time. Surely it's only natural to be influenced by a foreign experience, no matter how unimpressionable you think you are.

Wayne Costelloe was only in the starting blocks of his career, but already he had earned the respect of the teaching staff and the students at the college. Think about it! An Aborigine from Australia working in Phuket as a teacher, giving of himself to educate youngsters from another country. It was a sacrifice most people wouldn't even consider, but something Wayne didn't regard as a sacrifice, more as an inevitable part of his life. A destiny just waiting to be played out. I observed him over the four days, and learnt what this country had given to him, and what he'd given to it ... the two of them were so compatible.

"I think I've given them a broader knowledge of Australia,

and a broader knowledge of the history and people of Australia. And most importantly that I'm Aboriginal, and I am able to do this! To be a teacher in Thailand.

Thais call Aborigines in Australia, the "local people".

"From them I've gained a lot more patience, my world is wider now. I think I've become a more broad-minded person. It's taught me how to appreciate what I've got, because some of the conditions here are pretty desperate third world conditions. It's made me realise that I can do this, and I have done it, and I've done well."

There was, however, an unpretentious modesty about Wayne, as if all of this work in Phuket was no big deal. I guess because he was away from home and knee-deep in another culture, the significance of what he was doing had not fully crystallised. But for me, an outsider from eight thousand kilometres away, the impact he was having glowed brightly. I was so proud of him.

There was also a hint of irony about his position as a teacher. I wondered what his ancestors' reaction would be if they could see how Wayne was treated at the college. Having the students and the others bow to him, out of respect, wasn't exactly the way Aborigines had found things in Australia after the Europeans arrived. His ancestors would have laughed at such a thought. While to us the bowing might have a ring of subservience about it, Wayne saw it a little differently. For him, bowing was not a sign of superiority or inferiority. If someone bowed to him, he saw it as a mutual exchange of respect, acknowledging the existence of the other person. Here I saw someone at ease with himself, a confident and skilful communicator, with an appreciation of people and a deep concern for their welfare. He'd made them laugh and cry, but above all had taken most of his time, and given it to them. They used some of it to find out more about the Aborigines in Australia, or the "local people" as the Thais call them. It was all a sort of symbiosis.

One particular moment was worth the trip just for itself. The grapevine works pretty effectively at the college, because it wasn't too long before just about everyone knew there was a visitor at the school, and to top it off, he was another one of the "local people" from Australia. His name was also Waykin. And he had come all the way from Australia to see their teacher, so they wanted to see him. Wayne summoned me to his English class. All I had to do was tell these young folk something about my history, and answer their questions, he assured me.

The classroom was on the second level of the English faculty. The buildings were very basic, and looked run down, especially the toilet facilities. To their credit, though, the students looked a million dollars. Those forty young men and women in their mid- to late-teens, were all dressed in a black and white uniform and had taken some time with their grooming. I sat on a chair in front of them, and rambled on about why I was there, and some of my history.

That part of the class wasn't a real problem, but it was somewhat embarrassing when some of them only wanted to know my marital status, and would I sing a song for them about my home country. Nothing came to mind immediately thank goodness, so after a bit of persuasion they gave up on that idea. But I will always remember what followed.

Wayne had devised a lyp-sinc exercise for the students, where they had to sing along to an English language song to help their English presentation and communication skills, and also just to have a bit of fun. Now this was where they also reminded me so much of Aborigines. The way they teased each other was reminiscent of the way Aboriginal kids carry on. Their reactions to my visit reminded me of the times I'd been in front of Aboriginal school children: it was the same nervous shyness initially, which then turns into more of a showing off once they get used to you.

No one wanted to go first. It took about ten minutes of confusion before one group of five got up before the class, and started to sing along to the pop song Wayne played on a cassette.

But the best was saved for last. Wayne unexpectedly rose to his feet, inserted a cassette, and began to sing along to this love song, to wild screams of delight from the whole class. Then he grabbed one of the young girls by the hand, and led her up to the

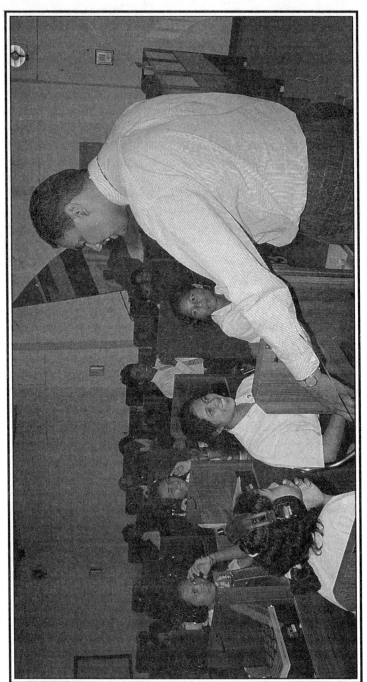

Wayne Costelloe entertaining his Thai students

front for a slow dance. This man let loose. He waltzed down the aisles, stopping now and again to lean over and sing a few words to a few of the girls. I couldn't believe what was going on. He put everything into this performance, and the students loved it. What a show stopper! Here was a special type of communicator. He could delight and surprise his students, and make them think.

It's a good feeling knowing you're Aboriginal, that you've always known from a young age that you are part of this special group of people in the world.

I hope I never lose the panavision of the children's faces, the striking countryside, or the wonderful camaraderie of this Aborigine and the Thai teenagers he taught at Phuket teachers college. Please let me lose a few other memories, to make sure this one stays in the foreground ... it's important to me. Wayne Costelloe was the first Aboriginal Australian Volunteer Abroad, so he had set another standard. But Wayne Costelloe was also just being himself, and if that helped change a few ideas about Aborigines, then all the better. "It's a good feeling knowing you're Aboriginal, that you've always known from a young age that you are part of this special group of people in the world."

When his father fell ill in Rockhampton, Wayne flew home and struggled with divided loyalties: return to Thailand or stay with his family. "I was talking to my dad in hospital, and he said, 'Go back over there and finish your work! Don't want them saying Murris can't stick anything out.' Both my mum and dad have always finished what they started in life. I think once Dad said it, the whole family accepted it as the right thing to do.

"I want to be an ambassador for Australia, working in a foreign country, because the world doesn't know much about Aborigines. They don't see us in positions of responsibility. I think by being there you're making an invaluable contribution to Aboriginal people and to all of society. For too long Aborigines have been seen as no-hopers, and people who are on training schemes the whole time, but never advance."

This twenty-eight-year-old has taken a step closer to his dream of becoming an ambassador. He applied to the Foreign Affairs Department for a cadetship while he was in his final year at Phuket in 1992. The two years in Thailand was a big plus for him, because he was accepted, and is now studying law and commerce at Griffith University in Brisbane. Waiting at the end of the five years is a job as a Professional Officer Grade 1 with the Department of Foreign Affairs and Trade.

Rhoda Roberts

TV PRESENTER-JOURNALIST

Cast your mind way back to that special day. A day that for some particular reason has never lost its intensity through the years. A moment or an event that will shine like no other. All of us will have it one day, and some will claim it as the reason why, as the turning point.

For Rhoda Roberts that day came in Lismore in Northern New South Wales when she was only fourteen years old. Nothing too exciting happened in the classroom on this day, but her moment wasn't far away. Her father had come to school to pick her up, and was waiting patiently in the car. This big Aboriginal man behind the steering wheel of his F.J. Holden, drew the attention of one of the young girls, who couldn't resist the temptation. "What do you call a boong who drives a car? A thief!" Rhoda heard the joke, and out of embarrassment for her father, and out of shame, hid behind some bushes, so they wouldn't associate her with this black man out in the car.

Although her father hadn't heard what went on, he suspected something was amiss when Rhoda jumped in. Frank Roberts was a Church of Christ minister, and understood his daughter and the problems Aboriginal children endured in everyday life. In his wisdom he then gave to Rhoda that special something which lifted her above and beyond her confusion. "Don't hide from who you are," he told her. "You can succeed if you're an Aborigine."

Segregation was disappearing in this country town, and at long last Aboriginal people could go to the pictures and swim in the local pool. The times were changing for the better all across Australia, and Frank Roberts impressed upon his daughter that she could be anything, and do anything she wanted with her life.

Up until then Rhoda had been torn by her feelings. While her parents instilled in her a great deal of self-confidence about her

Television presenter-journalist Rhoda Roberts at work

Aboriginality, and how unique she was, Rhoda was having all those feelings ripped apart by the pressure at school to compete against white students academically and socially.

We were told how wonderful and how special we were from Dad, but you'd go to school, and you'd be slotted into: 'You're a no hoper, you're lazy!'

"We were told how wonderful and how special we were from Dad, but you'd go to school, and you'd be slotted into: 'You're a no hoper, you're lazy!' I was constantly trying to prove myself. I had a lot of problems trying to keep up with the white peer pressure, because I used to set high goals. I wanted to prove I was as good as them. There were times when I'd come home and sit in the bath for hours with lemons, trying to get rid of my freckles and trying to be white."

Not anymore though! The impromptu sermon delivered to Rhoda in the car that week-day afternoon, suddenly put it all into perspective. She didn't have to compete, she was an individual, a person with intelligence and conviction. If she wanted it badly enough and worked at it, it was there for the taking. This has been the axis of her life since then, presenting to the world a woman with eclectic tastes and skills full of life, energy, and high ideals.

Her father gave her the gift of understanding her culture and who she was, while her mother Muriel gave the gift of strength. When she was a teenager, Rhoda was surprised to find out she actually wasn't royalty, despite her father continually proclaiming she was a princess of the Bunjalung people. That was the way it was back then. A family life radiating warmth and understanding, while outside that circle existed hatred and prejudice.

In the early to mid-sixties, when Rhoda was a little girl, parts of New South Wales were in a powder keg situation. It was Australia's little "deep south". Groups of Aborigines, following the example of the American civil rights movement, travelled on "freedom rides". They went by bus to towns full of racial hatred, sat with the townsfolk and tried to work out the problems. These freedom rides were also a strong sign of protest. It was an era of segregation and confrontation.

For some people, black and white, it left bitter memories of communities cut down the middle by colour barriers. Rhoda witnessed some of the racial frenzy her parents suffered. Frank Roberts was an Aborigine, and Muriel Roberts was a white woman, living under the same roof, a husband and wife in a volatile environment. As devout Christians, they endured the slurs, believing all along that someone of a higher order was leading the way. As they found out, even Christianity wasn't exempt from becoming infected with the disease. Rhoda's father wasn't accepted by some of the other ministers in the church, and the congregation wasn't about to be preached to by a black man. Yet in the same breath, these God-fearing people were supposed to be Christians. Her mother didn't get off that easy either.

"Living in a town like Lismore back in the fifties, sixties, and seventies, it didn't matter how fair skinned you were, if you had mixed parents, they drew a line, and said, 'You're a black person, full stop! You're not like us.'

"I think the worst racism I've ever known was the treatment of my mother. She came from a fairly middle class family, arrived in a country town like Lismore … I'm a twin, she had another child ten months older, and was pregnant again. At the time, my father was away. No one would talk to her until they sussed her out, and decided she wasn't 'white trash'.

"The strength of my mum has given me strength. I've been in Church when ministers have stood up and indirectly called my mum immoral, because she married a black man. There was my mum, head up, proudly walking out of church with us.

"My mother always made sure we were dressed up. We hated it, but she used to say, 'Outclass them! They think you're going to dress that way, show them that you're capable of dressing this way. If you outclass them, then they have to question.' That was her motto.

"By the time I was fifteen or sixteen, we were quite dark, and Mum was blonde and blue-eyed. Nothing gave us greater pleasure than to walk into a department store and have Mum at one end, and yell out 'Mum!' People would look at these kids. And they would come up and say, 'Oh what lovely children, did you adopt them? What a lovely kind woman.' When she'd say, 'No, they're my children from a mixed marriage', their whole attitude would change. She had to put up with an awful lot of that."

The Koorie community loved my mother. It was the white community that gave them hell.

When Muriel Roberts met her husband's family, they were living on an Aboriginal reserve in housing that could only be described as shanty dwellings. "You can imagine my mother walking in and thinking, 'Oh my goodness, I'm not bringing my children up like this!' She was a bit shocked, but after she got to know my grandparents and the Koorie ways, well, she was fine. She's a very brave woman. The Koorie community loved my mother. It was the white community that gave them hell."

While Rhoda wanted to tear the town apart with her bare hands, it was her parents who were the steadying influence, and you wouldn't expect anything else from two people who devoted their lives to the welfare of others. It did take a long time for some attitudes to change. Frank Roberts though was gaining a reputation as a charismatic preacher, reminiscent of the evangelists he had trained with in America. At long last he had an assembly of blacks and whites who respected him for his work. Racism was still endemic in the region, but in their own way, the Robertses had contributed immeasurably to the slow turnaround in public thinking.

"My father used to scare me! He was very charismatic with that evangelist, revival type of preaching. My father always used to relate it back to Aboriginal culture, when he did preach. On the way to church we would nick into the local shop and buy chocolate with our offering money. I used to sit there and think, he knows! He knows I spent that money."

The simple Christian values of "turn the other cheek" and "love thy neighbour" sounded so wonderful in principle, but were hard to come to terms with for Rhoda, when all else was caving in with hate. It would have been easy for her to become bitter, but when she thinks about those days, it was the two icons, her mother and father, who taught her how to question, to look much deeper for the reasons why, why some people hated Aborigines.

One of Rhoda's biggest joys in life was helping out at Lismore hospital on the school holidays. Her dream of becoming a nurse was shattered by a matron who refused Rhoda entrance to the general nurses' training because she was an Aborigine, even though her grades were better than others who applied. Once again with the guidance of her mother, Rhoda picked herself up, and headed off to Canterbury Hospital in Sydney, where she was accepted, and completed her training after three years of hard work.

This young, shy Aborigine who entered the working world in Sydney, emerged with a lot more self-assurance, and set out to discover herself and the world. She was a waitress and a nursing sister on the Barrier Reef's Hayman Island. Having saved enough money Rhoda went overseas to England, intending to stay for seven years.

A lot of people thought I was Spanish, Greek, Italian and when I went to those countries, people would come up and start speaking the lingo.

There Rhoda held a fascination for a lot of people simply because she was different from anyone they'd seen before. The skin and the looks weren't what they had come to imagine Aborigines really looked like, from what they saw on television.

"A lot of people thought I was Spanish, Greek, Italian and when I went to those countries, people would come up and start speaking the lingo."

In Europe's great cultural melting pot, Rhoda slotted into the lifestyle easily, unintentionally assuming the role as the exotic, but never failing to chastise those who were a little misguided about Aborigines. Rhoda's way of determining someone's sin-

Rhoda Roberts, SBS TV reporter

cerity in England's class dominated society was quite simple yet effective. She wouldn't divulge her heritage unless someone specifically asked. If there was a sudden change of attitude, this young firebrand wanted to know why. She didn't want to be prejudged because of her race, but by her strength of character. In Rhoda's case the latter usually won out.

The land which was at her very soul was pulling at her, sixteen thousand kilometres away, beckoning. Rhoda sees it as a spiritual thing that Aborigines can relate to; but most white Australians have trouble understanding, purely and simply, because they're landless, they're not indigenous to this country. The connotations of that are very real to Rhoda. Don't address her as an Australian, when that term means you're a derivative of another ethnic group, or you're Anglo-Saxon. She's an Aborigine, not an Australian. She is of this country, and if anything tied to Uluru, not to England and the Union Jack, or any other foreign country. To some it may seem pedantic, but it gives Rhoda her identity. There is Aboriginal blood running through her veins, which locks her irrevocably into the history and the future of this land, like no other.

The call was answered! Rhoda worked and saved tirelessly for about six months to come home, combining her job as a nurse at Westminster Hospital in London, with managing a restaurant. In 1985 after almost four years away Rhoda touched down on home soil, ready to turn another corner, and start a new chapter in her life.

That same year she auditioned for a part in the movie *The Fringe Dwellers*, but was unsuccessful. Rhoda had dabbled in some acting previously, but only on a small-time basis. Now she delved deeper into the performing arts world, and her first love, nursing, was pushed aside more and more. Here was a new direction, a new passion. "Do you want to get to the top? Well if you don't climb the mountain, honey, you'll never get there." Those words by her father many years ago were tattooed across her subconscious, driving Rhoda further and further.

With Lydia Miller, Justine Saunders and the late Vivian Walker, Rhoda co-founded the National Aboriginal Theatre Trust in Sydney. The stage for her was almost the last bastion for

Aboriginal comment in this country. The street marches and protest songs had all fallen by the wayside. Performances about Aborigines by Aborigines would offer white Australia a chance to get to know the indigenous people better.

"We have the opportunity to use subtle subtexts to get people to start thinking. We don't have to come down too heavy on them with the guilt trip, but help them to understand why some Aborigines drink, and why they feel dispossessed."

Her first big break into television came in 1989 when the ethnic television broadcaster SBS devised the "First in Line" series. It was the first national Aboriginal program. Rhoda applied for the job of presenter. Her dilemma was how to make the right impression. She drew on acting methodology at the audition, playing out the role of a presenter. It was no Oscar winning portrayal, and she was totally taken by surprise when the message came through, she'd be part of the team.

First things first though. The illusion she had cast at the interview wasn't the real Rhoda Roberts. She now had to realign her thinking on the wavelength of a serious week-in week-out presenter and reporter. Only experience and hands-on training could develop that, something she achieved in her year with the show. For Rhoda it was a privilege to begin with the prototype which gave the kick-start to everything else that's followed since: "Blackout" on ABC-TV, "Aboriginal Australia", and other Aboriginal programs.

There wasn't very much work around for Aboriginal actors, so Rhoda did some freelance media work. Then came an Australian satellite link-up for a worldwide environment program titled "Our Beautiful Planet". Rhoda Roberts' ad lib piece on the subject hit the people in the right places, and once again she was back at SBS, in the front seat job of the ethnic affairs program "Vox Populi". This time it was her ability not only her Aboriginality, that impressed the management.

And please, that's the way she wants it. Recognition as a good female presenter has taken the last ten years of climbing that mountain. She is tough and resilient, but you have to be in the television industry. Here's a young woman who can flit between the business suit world of the television social set to the earthy realism of Aboriginal communities, who is buoyed by her achievements so far, but always wary of the chameleon facade of her profession.

As an Aborigine who has straddled both the indigenous and the mainstream, Rhoda is optimistic about what lies ahead, yet cautious about the approach. She believes Aborigines should be reporting, acting, producing, and directing on a whole range of black and white issues.

It's great those Aboriginal units were set up, but I think we have to be really careful now that we just don't sit in our comfortable little blinkered boxes.

"A lot of people might hate me for this, but I just think we've got to be so careful. I know there's a need for Aboriginal units in broadcasting, but we have to start showing that as people working in television and radio, not only can we do Aboriginal things, but we can work in other genres as well. Otherwise we can become a little ghetto, and I really worry about that. It's great those Aboriginal units were set up, but I think we have to be really careful now that we just don't sit in our comfortable little blinkered boxes."

Talking to Rhoda makes you think: how far off is that day when we turn on our favourite soapie or drama, and actually see an Aboriginal person or family co-existing with the rest of the community in everyday situations? Heaven forbid, if you see an Aboriginal face on too many commercials in Australia ... now come on, how could anyone possibly imagine an indigenous person selling a product or endorsing one? Don't upset the apple cart! You'll confuse all those millions around the world, who have a clear definition of what Aborigines are, and the role they play in this their country. It's too late anyway isn't it? They'll never believe that Aboriginal lawyers, doctors, teachers, actors, and professionals work in Australia. How can they start to comprehend that notion if they haven't seen it on television? Just stick to what's been the formula so far. You know, the one where

Aborigines are continually the victims of society, entrenched in hopelessness and despair.

The perpetuation of the victim mentality by some of the media and other influences, is a contentious issue for Rhoda, but something she's trying to change. The biggest heartache is that its effect can be seen and felt across Australia, particularly among the youngsters, who've been brainwashed by it. The system has left some Aborigines virtually incapable of adjusting, because of drugs, alcohol, and total despair. Their survival lies in the hands of others.

Rhoda has strong views on the "victim mentality".

Where is this mentality coming from? We have to question it.

"To be Aboriginal you've got to be blacker than black, you've got to be a victim to be Aboriginal, you've got to drink to be Aboriginal, you've got to be hit by your man, cause only then you're an Aboriginal woman. Where is this mentality coming from? We have to question it. It upsets me when I know people who've got an education, but are just throwing it away to feel sorry for themselves.

"I just worry that the next generation is going to pick up this victim mentality, and it's a vicious cycle. We have to get away from that and start thinking for the future. Not this, 'Oh, if we put in the submission in July, we'll get the grant for next year!' No, start looking at self-sufficiency, start looking at an independent business."

Along with all the other Aboriginal high-fliers in similar positions around this country, Rhoda Roberts is political whether she likes it or not, political in the sense she has a great deal of influence as an actor and a presenter of a national television program. People listen to what Rhoda has to say, on subjects ranging from feminism to the rise and fall of Aboriginal languages. By her own steady persistence the public will be told about the inequalities in Australia. If there are those days when Rhoda hits rock bottom, a phone call to a close friend spurs her on. She also reflects on what her Aboriginal ancestors went through, and the absolute degradation and humiliation they suffered for her and others. She thinks about how they would be ashamed of the apathy this generation has fallen into. Rhoda has only to think about the blood spilled by those innocent people to once again feel humble and revived.

She is one of the few in the media, a select band of Aborigines given the task of clearing the path ahead. But she believes that community-based people who work in areas like land councils and schools, these people will change opinion more than the high-fliers. "There are far more important people than us."

In the forties they talked about assimilation, then it was integration, and now it's reconciliation.

But what of the future? Rhoda has a real problem with federal government efforts for "reconciliation". "In the forties they talked about assimilation, then it was integration, and now it's reconciliation."

They won't fool Rhoda with the camouflage of big words and fancy titles! There's a naked truth hidden between the pages of policy documents and ministerial jibberish, that's all too clear to her. When the outer layers are stripped off, what is left are two different cultures. Now forget about one nation living segregated from the other, because what Rhoda draws from that conclusion is they can both live, and prosper in Australia, but only when the scales of justice rest evenly.

Make no mistake, Rhoda can see black and white reconciled in her country in some manner in the future, however she believes this process of reconciliation aimed at the year 2001 to coincide with the centenary of federation is simply political froth and bubble, with absolutely no substance. Her greatest fears have been substantiated: the government is still not listening to what Aboriginal people are telling them. "Another ten years to find out what the problems are. What a load of rubbish. We've been saying that the fundamental issues — health, education, etcetera

— are the problem, and it all comes from the one source. And that is Aborigines were never recognised as the sovereign owners of this country, and that our history books are still getting it wrong."

She wants the point made succinctly to those wise folk hanging around the corridors of Parliament House in Canberra. The message, ladies and gentlemen, is to stop perpetuating the handout syndrome, and forget about the hundreds and millions of dollars over a decade, in what only really amounts to political glorification. Instead simply use some of it to get the text books off the shelves, and re-write the correct history of Australia! Then and only then will change occur. If they can re-publish the nursery rhymes and other literature without the racist inferences, then the precedent has been set.

Mention a Republic and Rhoda admits she has not got all the answers. But she believes it can not happen until the issue of sovereignty is addressed and Aboriginal and Torres Strait Islander people are recognised as the sovereign people of this nation.

While she supports political organisations such as the Aboriginal Provisional Government, she feels there is still a need for Aboriginal political parties on the same lines as the Greens or Independents, reflecting the diversity and various interests of all Aborigines. Although uncertain about politics, Rhoda says one thing is certain — "As young Aborigines we must listen to our elders and respect their judgment, and always listen to the community at grass roots level."

"Senator" Rhoda Roberts doesn't sound too far out of place, does it? Rhoda has thought about it for a long time, with more than just a passing interest. There must be an Aborigine in the system who's sensitive to the issues and in touch with the people. It doesn't make sense to her that other indigenous cultures have had their candidates sitting in office for years, making the changes or pushing for them. Yet until this day Neville Bonner is the only Aboriginal federal parliamentarian Australia has produced.

However, for the moment Rhoda is already busy enough. Apart from fronting "Vox Populi", she does some part-time radio work, is writing a book and a play, and has the hazy outline of a movie script. With longtime friend Lydia Miller, Rhoda runs a media/theatre consultancy business, AMPIMEDIA.

Communication was a real stumbling block for this naturally shy young lady, but now it has turned into an addiction. She wants to entertain, on television, the big screen, or the stage, and to educate at the same time. It has been an amazing swingshift, from those apprehensive days in Lismore to the heights of a national profile. She keeps coming back to communication now, no matter what life throws at her.

The death of her father in 1992 gave Rhoda more focus to her life. First priority is her widowed mother, whose unconditional commitment and love can probably never be repaid. But she's going to try anyway, by one day buying a farm on Bunjalung land. Success for Rhoda is her land under her feet, the family next to her, and all the warmth and support that goes with it.

Pastor Frank's daughter is very near the top of that mountain.

Ernie Dingo

ACTOR

Where do I begin with someone like Ernie Dingo? This most talented man, who has delighted Australians for the last decade or so, is ... whatever you want him to be! Should I tell you first about his personality, how he simply takes you by the hand, and leads the way. It's like he's the conductor, and you're the orchestra, just waiting patiently for the signals to follow.

From the moment I jumped in Ernie's car, everything was a lot of fun, and everyone was fair game. There was a comical routine in just about anything, including the crazy drivers we passed as we drove around Sydney. Ernie was rehearsing in a small hall with the Bangarra Dance Theatre at Redfern for the Mo entertainment awards. It's amazing how you expect people to be a certain way, with those little images you build up in your subconscious. Ernie Dingo was all of those things, funny, charming, but above all a natural person.

It was a great afternoon watching how easily those Aboriginal performers combined the traditional and contemporary dance styles. Even in rehearsal they made me feel as if I should have paid at the door, because of the quality show they put on! Ernie's role in the six-minute piece was a sixty-second didgeridoo introduction, which would have been worth the price of admission on its own. His musicianship is one part of his repertoire that isn't spoken about too often, but he uses the instrument as if it is an extension of himself. He can make that woodwind do almost anything he wants.

Originally the organisers of the awards had asked for his services only, however Ernie convinced them to go beyond that and promote just a little more of the abundance of Aboriginal talent on offer not only in Sydney, but around Australia. It is something he's been promoting for a long time, for people to realise he's not the only Aboriginal performer who's capable of

Entertainer Ernie Dingo on the basketball court at Redfern in Sydney getting up in front of an audience and wowing them. And a change is happening in that way, but not fast enough, and white Australia is the loser.

Ernie Dingo has blazed a trail not only for himself, but just as importantly for Aboriginal people in this country. His stepfather once told him not to contemplate things for too long: he could have the job done in the time he spent thinking about it. "My boy just get in there and do it!" Those words have stuck with Ernie through everything he's accomplished since those early days back in 1979 when he stepped on stage before his first audience. On the advice of his best friend Richard Walley, Ernie auditioned for the roles of Yagan and Jamie Yoragh in a Jack Davis play titled *Kullark*. It was at the Playhouse Theatre in Perth, and Ernie was twenty-three years old.

He loved the stage, but it was a game for him. For the next few years Ernie was an Aboriginal cultural officer in Melbourne, teaching at a race relations camp. Then he toured Australia with another Jack Davis production, *Dreamers*, in 1982, in which he had the role of Eli Wallach. He loved it so much that at twenty-five Ernie Dingo chose Sydney, and acting. The first few years were tough and full of stereotyped roles.

There aren't enough scripts around for black people in Australia. We need a lot more Aboriginal material done.

"There aren't enough scripts around for black people in Australia. We need a lot more Aboriginal material done. It's the old adage: there's no money in black money."

But Ernie got on. And appeared in *The Fringe Dwellers, State of Shock* and *Tudawali*. These films dealt with Aboriginal social problems, but through the eyes of a white producer, white director, and white film script. Ironically in the bicentennial year of 1988, Ernie Dingo won the AFI best actor award for a television production, "Waltz Through the Hills". At long last Aborigines weren't token members of the industry. This coveted prize from the Australian Film Industry was not only for Ernie.

He accepted it in recognition of those who were there much earlier, actors like Justine Saunders and David Gulpilil, who inspired him.

It was the television comedy "Fast Forward" that helped to make Ernie Dingo a household name. He has also appeared in "Dearest Enemy" and "Dolphin Cove" on TV. His international credits in *Crocodile Dundee II* and *Until the End of the World* have expanded the cinema profile of Aborigines.

There were many pleasing aspects of *Until the End of the World*. Firstly the chance to work in France. Secondly it was a part where the Aboriginal tag was not attached: "I play an Australian detective and there's no reference to his Aboriginality until near the end of the movie where he discovers he was taken away from his people when he was young." Thirdly, he was delighted to work with Oscar-winning actor William Hurt. He learnt the technique of "blocking out" from Hurt — how to "block out" the noise and chaos of a shoot, and concentrate on your part. Ernie was impressed with Hurt: "He might be fussing about this and that like most stars do, and having a tiff with the leading lady, but as soon as that little red light comes on, you'd swear he was in love with that woman."

But if ever there was a production which highlighted his acting skills, and all the other strands of his talents, then the 1990 stage show *Bran Nue Dae* was it. Written by Jimmy Chi and a collective of Aboriginal talent living around Broome in Western Australia, it holds pride of place for Ernie. The role of Uncle Tadpole offered to the Australian public the rare sight of Ernie Dingo acting, singing, dancing, and playing the comic all rolled up into one. I saw it in Brisbane, and marvelled at Ernie's style. The young Aborigines who were making their debut simply took my breath away with their professionalism. It was just so good, and a genuine advertisement for indigenous creativity ... a play with the word Aborigine stamped all over it, from the original music, to the performers, to the writing. An Australian play addressing important issues, but also having a bit of fun.

Ernie believes Aborigines understand what it is like to be black as well as white. On the other hand he doesn't think white Australia has got much concept of what it's like to be black. He doesn't think many have experienced racism, and been forced to live on the outside in their own country. "Aborigines have suffered so much negativity towards our culture and our life, and yet we still don't know what it is like to hate. It shows that we're more humane than some of these other people will ever be. If you want to understand about humanity, just check out the indigenous people all over the world.

"You can go to a black community area and everybody will want to have a talk with you to say hello, or acknowledge you as they're passing. You go into the city at lunch time and everybody's in their own world. A million people. If I'm in the city I like to say hello and smile at people. *What's that black person want? ... What's he so happy about? ... Why is he looking at me?*

White people look at blacks and think of alcohol, fighting, racism, no education, dirty. They don't want to learn about the complexities of an Aboriginal person, they don't want to accept that we're just as good as them.

"We've never been trained to be ourselves. We basically are becoming stereotype whites. But you know the white society isn't our society. Our society comes from togetherness, and we don't have to be acceptable coons. If we be ourselves that's more honest. We're faced with a lot of negativities throughout every day, just by the colour of our skin. Sometimes it's positive, and a lot of times it's negative. White people will see a black person and think of all the reasons why there are black people. Yet black people can look at white people, and try to work out where they're from. Whether they're Irish or whatever. White people look at blacks and think of alcohol, fighting, racism, no education, dirty. They don't want to learn about the complexities of an Aboriginal person, they don't want to accept that we're just as good as them."

However, Ernie believed that white domination over the past two centuries had poisoned the minds of some of his people, so that they had more animosity for their own people than anyone else. Coming face to face with all that pent up pain hurt him.

"I was in Brisbane a while ago, and this bloke had a few too many beers. He had his fist up against my throat, threatening me. He said, 'Ernie Dingo, I'll punch you.' I said to him, 'Hey Bros, where I come from we hit! If you've got an argument with me, take your shirt off, and I'll take you outside, as long as we get it out in the open. And as soon as we finish I'll have a beer and a yarn with you.' I told him he should have more respect for me anyway. He said, 'Why, because you're an actor and a big shot? You should have respect for *me*. This is my country up here! Queensland is my country.' I said to him, 'Hey Cous, you should have respect for me, because I had the decency to get out of my country, and come and visit yours.' "

The only time I wish I was white, is at three o'clock in the morning trying to catch a cab.

That was a real life situation which he will probably transform into a comedy routine. Ernie's law is simple: Aborigines are able to laugh at themselves. Ernie has been doing it for years in his comedy acts: *The only time I wish I was white, is at three o'clock in the morning trying to catch a cab ... The positive thing about being black is jumping on a bus during peak hour, and getting to have a whole seat to yourself.*

"I was doing a routine one night, and there was one guy in the back who was slinging off about Aborigines, saying, 'Oh! That was a good nigger joke that one." He carried on with this, so I said, 'that's all right, brother, I'll deal with you in a minute.' All of a sudden he yells out, 'Hey, I'm not your brother!' So I yelled back at him, 'Well who knows where your grandfather has been mate, because we could be related.' Everybody laughed ... and he felt so embarrassed, he shut up.

"If you get some radical person in the audience, you tell him or her, 'Look if you really want to understand Aboriginal people, you go for a walk, and you start to think about yourself. Walk five kilometres in the morning, and five kilometres in the evening. By the end of the week you should be at least seventy kilometres away. Now go away!'

"I knock back a lot of scripts. I won't do a lot of scripts, because basically they're written by Toorak people writing what they think are black jokes.

I take black jokes and put them to the front, I'm not afraid of laughing at myself, at Aborigines, because I am Aboriginal!

"I take black jokes and put them to the front, I'm not afraid of laughing at myself, at Aborigines, because I am Aboriginal! I don't laugh at white people, because I'm not white. You have a look at some comedy productions, they're laughing at the deformities or abnormalities of other people. I mean they laugh at gays, at lesbians, they laugh at fat people, they laugh at everybody except themselves. Laughing at others less fortunate than yourself isn't an Aboriginal trait, but more a sign of weakness. It shows a lack of understanding of the world and humanity. That's why I can't work in an area where I have to laugh at other people, where I have to show a negative side to black people. There's too much negative things on black people as it is."

A sketch Ernie wrote called "Yuppy's Auction: Living Next Door to a Black Fella" had a real cutting edge. A yuppy house auction became a farce after prospective buyers were deterred by the prospect of living next door to an Aboriginal family. Little did they know, they'd been set up by these Aborigines, who exposed the hidden racism for quite selfish means ... to lower the price so they could afford it themselves. In the space of a few minutes, Ernie not only made people laugh, but hopefully stirred some consciences.

"Some blacks say it's too embarrassing doing those routines publicly, that I get a little close to the bone when I'm on stage. They say I got no shame standing up there talking about black people like that in front of a lot of whites! But I say, 'Hey Brother, did you laugh?' 'Yes, but ...' they say."

He believes Aboriginal comedy is the best comedy in Australia. Ernie has heard some of the funniest things in the pub with the boys, or sitting around the barbecue on a Saturday night. The only trouble is they won't get up on stage with that material, so Ernie often uses it in his stage performances.

In Australian television drama, however, the problem still remains that the parts for Aborigines are a shallow reflection of a non-Aboriginal view.

Racism stems from what you see on TV. Not seeing an Aboriginal family in these productions is part of that.

"White Australians basically are racist. Racism stems from what you see on TV. Not seeing an Aboriginal family in these productions is part of that. It's all right to have a black American family in there, that's fine, but not a black Australian. But you can't paint a black picture, if you only use white paint."

Ernie would like all Australians, black and white, to work together. "We have to get each other's hands dirty, by doing things physically together. All the talk in the world isn't going to help. We have to get down and dig dirt together."

This way, he believed, we would build a more prosperous future for everyone, where Aborigines would be given a little more elbow room and respect, in recognition of what they've given to Australia over thousands of years ... where the needs and desires of Aboriginal culture would be allowed to stand alongside that of the other societies in this country.

"Aboriginal people have been giving all the time. That's why we haven't got any bloody land left! It's in the nature of our lifestyle to give. But in a white situation, it's material gain, personal gain ... what's mine is mine, and what's your's will be mine ... divide and conquer.

"If Australia got a new flag, the appropriate one supposedly would be the Aboriginal flag, because it represents this land. But you can't imagine someone from Toorak or Bellevue Hill flying the black red and yellow out the front of their place."

It mystified him that the so-called "pioneers of the frontier",

Ernie Dingo away from the spotlight, at home in Sydney

like Lawson and Blaxland, and Burke and Wills, are given all the glory as the explorers who opened up the country. "They did have Aboriginal help, and quite a lot of it.

We have streets and towns named after other so-called heroes who have gone out and rid the land of blacks.

"We have streets and towns named after other so-called heroes who have gone out and rid the land of blacks. They are heroes as far as the white community is concerned."

Recognition is the key word. Until the original owners of this land are officially recognised by Australia, until people accept there are two separate cultures in Australia — those that have and those that have not — Ernie cannot see any form of reconciliation.

He's seen it so often all around the world, from Europe to his own area in Western Australia, where, he says, the Aborigines are used for labour and for sport: "It's so funny to go to a football game, and watch my brothers get out of their car, and the white fellas get out of theirs, and no one says anything to each other until they walk into the same club room, and put the same colour jumper on. When they're out on the field they pat each other, and back one another up all the time! But as soon as the match is finished, and they've showered, and put their civvies back on, they go in two separate directions, whether they win, lose or draw. And that's sad. It's sad that people should have those ideas about life."

I remember driving down the highway at about 140 kilometres an hour. Black night, no moon. I turned the lights off.

When he looks out across the land to where some of his people are, thousands of miles away, he thinks about all the changes since he was there, he thinks about the rising number of black deaths in custody. Ernie knows if he had stayed in the west, he might have become a victim.

He isn't one hundred percent guaranteed of his reaction to anything if he was lost to drugs and alcohol. Would you be able to endure a cold dark empty cell? And what would be going through your mind? Every time he hears of a black death in custody it tears him apart. "I remember driving down the highway at about 140 kilometres an hour. Black night, no moon. And raining. And thinking what it'd be like if I had no light. I turned the lights off. Oh hell, turn them back on, it's dark! Two seconds of darkness on a rainy night at that speed is crazy! And people don't know I've done that. It was a split second decision. And I did it! Now I'm not saying those people who died in jail did a similar thing, but all I'm saying is we don't always know! Some police are trying real hard, and sure, I realise some aren't."

Black deaths in custody is only one part of the suffering Aboriginal people carry around with them every day of their lives. No matter what, Ernie will continue to put Aboriginal people first. However, there's a longing in his voice and in his eyes, that tells of a refuge where there was no pain, hate or racism: his own world of red dirt and blue skies, where a young boy roamed freely across the country learning about his culture, and becoming one with it. Days he wished would last forever. Ernie can see them now clearer than ever. The wonderful unity of all the family together, all the uncles, aunties, nieces and nephews, and of course the image of his mother, the brightest star amongst all of them.

Ernie remembers that no one seemed to give a damn about the colour of anyone's skin, as long as they all did their job. Life was pretty good.

He was born on a cattle station called Bullardoo in the Murchison River region of Western Australia, some four hundred kilometres north of Perth. The family moved from station to station, working as cooks and domestics, until they settled in Mullewa. Wudjadi is his language, and he learnt it from a very early age. Ernie still speaks it today. He has great memories of his youth, simply because he encountered nothing but good will. Ernie remembers that no one seemed to give a damn about the colour of anyone's skin, as long as they all did their job. Life was pretty good. The station masters took advantage of the Aboriginal families as far as the wages were concerned, but there was a good relationship between the two, built on a mutual trust. The history of that region was remarkably devoid of any massacres or forced removal of Aboriginal children.

"There was always a job for the young people. If a young boy went to town and messed up, the station master always told the families, 'Any of them young boys down town not doing anything, bring them back. I'll have a job for them here.' They did look after us, so that's why I don't have that much hate inside me. Growing up with those people around you, you didn't really worry about black-white relationships. You were just like one mob from that area.

I'd like to go back to those first fifteen years of my life, go back to where everybody didn't give a damn whether you were black or white, male or female.

"I'm at the stage now where I'd like to go back to those first fifteen years of my life, go back to where everybody didn't give a damn whether you were black or white, male or female. We were just a bunch of people who worked together. That's what I remember mostly about my youth. We all pitched in."

Young Ernie Dingo wallowed in the paradise he knew. Everything was perfect for him, except for maybe one particular thing that used to bug him a bit. His stepfather was a boxer, and Ernie's three younger brothers had the same urge. But pugilistic power wasn't for this young fellow, as he soon found out. He dreaded boxing day when the ring was set up, and all the other Aboriginal boys in the town went slap happy mad. Didn't anyone understand Ernie Dingo was a pacifist? There was one fellow who always used to end up in the ring with Ernie. He got tired of beating Ernie up, so he would send in his brother. They could never work out why Ernie didn't fight back. Today after all those beatings, the three of them are good friends, and laugh about those days. They once remarked that Ernie was now famous all over the world. Ernie's reply was "You're famous too! Cause I told everyone you both used to beat me up as a kid."

He was funny, cheeky, friendly, and always had the perfect comeback to any question.

So boxing was definitely out as a career. Ernie wanted to be a stockman, just like his uncles. Then a bush fireman, then a sign-writer. The larrikin in him was always there, but at Geraldton High School it burst onto the scene like a thunderclap from the heavens, striking almost everyone, and drawing them all inextricably closer and closer. Whenever a new black kid came to Geraldton High, they eventually fell under his spell, joining the ever growing band of Aborigines and white kids this young rogue had gathered. How could you not be enticed. He was funny, cheeky, friendly, and always had the perfect comeback to any question. And he wasn't a bad athlete either. He won senior level state selection in basketball and in Australian Rules during the seventies, and he still keeps a spectator's eye on the sports.

Ernie moved to Perth after high school to become an apprentice sign-writer, and to join one of the bigger baseball clubs. Baseball was given over for basketball, and just when he was so close to finishing his apprenticeship his emotions got in the way. Downtown Perth on a Friday and Saturday night twenty years ago was much the same as it is today. The faces have changed, but the black and white mixture of drugs, alcohol, violence, and street kids hasn't. Ernie Dingo was embroiled in the middle of that in the early seventies, not as a player, but as a concerned friend. One day, when one of the kids was taken away to Longmore Juvenile Detention Centre, Ernie became a lot more than just concerned. All personal ambitions were put aside, and he began working at the centre as a prison officer. Ernie got on well with these young kids.

In 1977 he began residential child care work in order to get qualifications. But after a while, Ernie could not cope with the rigidity of the system. He broke away and instead went to work one-on-one with those troubled teenagers, and he hasn't stopped since.

Aboriginal people are so special because we understand a lot more that goes on around us. We see a lot more, we hear a lot more, we feel a lot more, we touch a lot more, and we taste a lot more.

The love of his people, of the earth, are the same. The dreams he has now are the ones he saw a long time ago. Every day is a new discovery about the wonderment of being an Aborigine. "Aboriginal people are so special because we understand a lot more that goes on around us. We see a lot more, we hear a lot more, we feel a lot more, we touch a lot more, and we taste a lot more, than the people around us. We have a panoramic vision of what's behind us, what's underneath us, and what's on top of us." It is all part of the cycle Ernie Dingo is engulfed in, where the land, the values, and traditions rotate around him, giving him all the energy he needs.

His world isn't a defined structure of money, prestige, and influence. What he's entwined in, is a much stronger force which goes on and on and on! It was given to him by his mother, from her mother, from her mother's mother … and so it goes!

"Every time I do an opening night it's for my mum and for my grandmother, and for all my family from the past, the present, and for the future.

"Wherever I go, if I go overseas, I take paints and paper with me. When I'm sitting down in my hotel room reminiscing about home, I'll paint home, and put those paintings up around the inside of my room. Cleaners come in and say, 'Wow! That's lovely! I say 'You want it? That's where I come from.' They want to buy it. But I say 'No, no, no, I can't sell you my land, I can't sell you my painting. This is my country, where

I come from. If you want it, you take it.' I paint pictures of bush scenes of home, all the soft colours. I take my Aboriginality with me all the time."

Maroochy Barambah and her daughter Baringa

Maroochy Barambah

OPERA SINGER

It's a voice…a sound that'll take hold. You hear it, and all you
want to do is enjoy it over and over again! I only wish more
people were in the hall on that morning to share the moment with
me. Maroochy Barambah shook me from way down below to
right up top.

On a windy weekend morning in Sydney, I wandered into a
building where there were a few people, a piano, and a striking
Aboriginal woman about to rehearse a new production. There
was nothing special about the surroundings, nothing to give
anything away about what was to follow. I had heard some of
her recordings before, and read some of the reviews about her
performances, but things like that never seem to prepare you for
a live experience.

I kept wondering if I should clap madly after each song. I
never know what to do in situations like that.

I was caught with the way she moved around the piano
motioning this way and that, and all the time reaching for the
right note, and the feel of the music. Afterwards it dawned on
me, the sensation I had wasn't from the present, but something
Maroochy and I share from a long time ago, a connection only
a few in this country are able to tap into…all up, it only lasted a
few hours, however it was more than ample time, to have it
finally confirmed. This woman is good, very good!

Whatever Maroochy Barambah has achieved in life so far, it
all relates back to the beginning, back to the days in Queensland
where she grew up as Yvette Isaacs. She's a "Sherbie", a mission
girl from Cherbourg, and a descendant of the Gubbi Gubbi
people.

At the settlement she jived with the other girls to the rock and
roll songs they saw on TV's "Bandstand". At twelve she tear-
fully said goodbye to her friends and her Aboriginal mission

childhood. She was the first Aborigine to graduate from the Victorian College of the Arts. Now she is on the brink of becoming an opera star. And her Aboriginality has had everything to do with her success.

I don't know what was in the water at Cherbourg Aboriginal Settlement, but this relatively small reserve near Kingaroy in southeast Queensland has produced the first male and female Aboriginal opera singers to appear professionally on stage. Many years before Maroochy, Harold Blair was an imposing figure on and off the stage, a man who was deeply committed to his family and his people. As a classically-trained concert singer, he toured extensively in Australia and overseas. He trained in Melbourne at the Melba Conservatorium and worked under Hector Crawford. He reached acclaim with his singing in Europe, but back in his own country, Harold Blair was never given the opportunities afforded to others with similar talents.

Maroochy Barambah was to benefit from this great man but when she was very young, and answered to the name Yvette Isaacs, all types of music made an impression on her. There was singing everywhere in this settlement in the fifties and sixties. Little wide-eyed Yvette would sit listening spellbound by the traditional singing, the wailing of the elders when someone passed away, the singing of hymns by her uncle in the A.I.M. church.

What else could she do except join in? Even scrubbing out the dormitories with her friends, especially on those cold winter mornings, became more tolerable when they all broke into song.

Mrs Clarke, the choir teacher, was the first person to offer Yvette a lead role, although at the time this eleven year old wasn't interested in what was going on. She was too busy day-dreaming, looking out the window during choir practice. Yvette was sort of there and sort of wasn't, but Mrs Clarke was impressed with what she heard, and that's all that mattered.

No one back then at the Cherbourg Aboriginal Settlement, including Yvette, had any idea where she would be twenty-five years later. "I'm proud I'm from CAS," the children sang, a lovely tune, and one that was taught to them very early on. The instructions were very clear: remember to be proud of your mission, and when you sing it, sing it with plenty of sincerity. Cherbourg was considered a role model settlement in Queensland in the fifties and sixties. When visitors arrived, Yvette and the other children were told: "Have a smile on your face, and don't forget to sing that little number to show your appreciation of all the fine work that's been done for you, and the reserve. We want our visitors to go away safe in the knowledge that the government is looking after you."

Not only could Yvette handle a gospel number with refined maturity, but as other influences started to creep in, she became pretty good with some of the rock and roll music on the radio. In the mid-sixties, in the big shed at the back of the dormitory every Saturday afternoon, Yvette and the girls used to line up on a make-believe stage and hit it! They watched "Bandstand" on television, and then imitated the go-go dancers ... Aboriginal girls all in a row, with arms and legs going this way and that! What a crazy sight! Come to think of it, I was doing something similar with the lads somewhere back then, imitating the rock and roll bands and their risque performances. I'd like to think Yvette was more believable than I was. She recalled those days with humour: "Being a church environment, you weren't supposed to sing songs of the world which you heard on the radio. But we'd sing them anyway, and say 'God forgive us' before we sang them! We knew we were doing the wrong thing, but we still wanted to do it."

I'd always been told before I even left
Cherbourg to be proud of my Aboriginality.

There was never any chance of forgetting who she was, and where she came from. "I'd always been told before I even left Cherbourg to be proud of my Aboriginality." Certain people made sure of that. Her mother was of Aboriginal, Scottish, and Ceylonese descent, a strong lady, who spent many years away from her daughter, working as a cook on cattle stations throughout Queensland. Spiritually though, the two were never apart, despite the distance between them...a powerful mother-dau-

ghter relationship, based on its Aboriginality, and all that went
with it.

During the years at the settlement, Yvette had gone away for
holidays to Melbourne. On occasions, she spent a few weeks
with a non-Aboriginal family. It was a special project initiated
by Harold Blair, which gave Aboriginal children the chance to
learn about another culture, and to expand their knowledge and
thinking. Then in 1968 — a year after a national referendum gave
Aborigines the right to vote — Yvette went south again, this time
not for a holiday, but to start a new life with a new family. Just
a teenager, she was about to break through the protective wall of
Cherbourg.

There was no way to hold back the tears. Yvette sat on the
plane wanting so badly to run down the aisle, and back to her
family. There was someone there to help her through it though.
He talked about life on Cherbourg and what lay outside. No one
could know how special that moment was when little Yvette
Isaacs and Harold Blair sat together on that flight south.

The next five years of Yvette's life were tough. Apart from
holidays, she hadn't known too much about the real world
outside the mission. While she had been well cared for at the
settlement, this young lady was intelligent enough to realise if
you were black you were at a disadvantage. She was proud of
her heritage, but always mindful of her place around white
people, because that's what she saw, and that was the example
her people, young and old, had set.

In Melbourne, she was fighting herself. This young girl was
blossoming into a young woman...and there was a battle with
that. Also, Yvette was now being pampered by white people...another new and rather confusing experience. Not only was
all of this a heavy burden but the thing Yvette needed most was
denied her. She hungered for anything to do with her race. She
needed to be reminded now and again of her people. But she
could find no books written by Aborigines, no radio programmes
about Aborigines, and no television shows on Aborigines. No
one could provide what she needed most, because anglicised
Australia was still unaware Aborigines had any culture. Her
foster parents were kind and caring, but had no idea Aboriginal

traditions were essential to her well being. Even the word "Aborigine" was rarely mentioned at the private school she attended.

"My foster parents were very good people, but they just didn't understand what was going on. They discouraged me, they didn't encourage me to know about my Aboriginality. They were products of the mentality of the time, you know. *Help the poor wretched darkies*. They thought what they were doing was the best thing, but in some ways it was destructive to Aborigines. But, I fought for my rights, and I knew how to be proud of being Aboriginal."

Yvette's next foster family sent her to Bonbeach State High School in Chelsea, where she was introduced to racism. The students let her know she was an intruder with the wrong coloured skin. As the only Aborigine at the school she was on her own. The rejection hurt her deeply, but this young Cherbourg spirit was tough, and she'd developed another dimension to her character. Like her father, she was never afraid to speak her mind. Yvette didn't retreat. Instead she came out declaring the advantages of being black and how special it made her feel. They were the occasions when she drew on Cherbourg for the strength to make it. She had been taught to be patient with others, and to carry with her the dignity of the Gubbi Gubbi. It was with her in Melbourne alright in the late sixties, but she wanted so badly to be back at Cherbourg. The family and friends she thought about almost every day of the week were just so far away, hundreds of kilometres from this wintry place.

As the years passed, Yvette and Melbourne grew closer. She came to love Australian Rules football, and in particular Richmond footy club. Like many Aboriginal children, she had played sport since an early age, athletics being a real love of hers, as well as basketball and rugby league. With sport, and a few loyal friends, Yvette began to mould into the lifestyle. There were still a few racial problems at school, but Yvette was adjusting. Four years passed since that plane trip south, and the tender twelve-year-old was now a socially aware teenager of the seventies. School was over, things were happening all around the world, and Yvette was a part of it.

Even today, 1972 is a year that is special for Maroochy. There were fledgling Aboriginal protests, the polarisation of Australia over the Vietnam War, and women's liberation. These events produced a woman more passionate about her Aboriginality and her womanhood. Melbourne felt like the epicentre. And there was music, wonderful music. Yvette boarded with a folk singer. "We just got talking one day, and she said, 'What would you like to do?' I said, 'Sing, I suppose!' She was organising a women's electoral lobby concert and that's when I started singing professionally. My first performance was at the Melbourne town hall."

I had to go back into my community in search of my Aboriginality.

The group toured Sydney and Canberra. Yvette was dedicated to the cause, but she didn't take singing all that seriously back then. Aretha Franklin and Marvin Gaye were her idols. All the energy of the civil rights movement, as well as the soul and blues accompaniment, was stirring Yvette. It was like a rich tapestry of promise and enlightenment. It was acceptable, and it was black. It made her yearn for her own culture. "I had gained a lot of good, positive things from my foster family. But it was a very crippling environment, very much as far as my Aboriginality was concerned. So I had to go back into my community in search of my Aboriginality."

She knew Cherbourg wouldn't be the same to her, after everything that had happened in the last few years. What her loved ones saw when she arrived for the Christmas holiday break in 1972 wasn't the little girl who had left. Here was someone who wasn't prepared to stand behind anyone, despite being black and a woman as well. In her heart, Cherbourg would always be her home, but there was a reason for being sent out into the world, and Yvette had to find it. At the same time she was saying hello, it was also goodbye. As she strolled around the reserve, it was obvious the answers weren't there! Spiritually the two were bonded completely, and nothing could ever come between them. These same forces, however, had led Yvette down another road, towards the now famous Aboriginal "tent embassy" protest outside Parliament House in Canberra. An Afro-haired Yvette was there, singing and marching.

She sang blues and jazz while working in various jobs around Melbourne. Then curiosity drew her into the performing arts world, and she enrolled in black theatre workshops and joined a traditional Aboriginal dance group. In 1976, she began to study classical music at the Melba Conservatorium of Music. The dean of the conservatorium suggested she would become a fantastic opera singer one day, but Yvette was young, and still unsure what direction to take. If only she had continued with that degree, it might all have happened sooner. After only a year she left to study drama at the Victorian College of the Arts, and three years later she was the college's first Aboriginal tertiary graduate.

She won roles in the successful and popular television productions "Winner Take All" and "Women of the Sun", but again and again it was the stereotyped "black girl" role she was offered. The need to prove people wrong about Aborigines was building. Yvette wanted to play her part in the transition, where "Aborigines won't be regarded as an oddity any more".

If that was ever to happen, Yvette felt there had to be a change somewhere. To assert herself as an artist, she needed a name, and of course it had to be Aboriginal.

Growing up in white Australia in the sixties, all you ever got was Anglo-Saxon women on the television, and just about everywhere else.

"Growing up in white Australia in the sixties, all you ever got was Anglo-Saxon women on the television, and just about everywhere else.

"I read about the legend of Maroochy, but it came to me in a dream as well. There is a story of a girl who turns into a swan in the Aboriginal legends of the Gubbi Gubbi people. And to me the swan, especially the Australian swan, which is black, is a symbol of black beauty. And that's what I wanted to be, as an

Maroochy captivating the audience at the Rockhampton Music Bowl

artist. It's a symbol of appreciating the beauty of Aboriginal women."

The word Maroochy is also the name of her tribal area, which ranges from Bribie Island to Fraser Island on Queensland's Sunshine Coast. Barambah Station is the old name for Cherbourg.

Maroochy's name not only represented her future plans but also took from her past, in remembrance of friends and loved ones brainwashed into believing what they were continually told about Aborigines, those who weren't able to take any steps forward. Alcoholism and despair ate away at their heritage. Some of Maroochy's singing partners from the dormitory days and Saturday afternoons in the shed will never see her perform. They are fallen victims Maroochy will never forget.

I love people no matter what colour they are. I don't think hate or anger corrects anything, it turns a lot of people off.

She also remembers some of the old stories told by her grandfather, who was a song man. He told her that many of her ancestors were wiped out at a poisoned waterhole. It has not left her angry about white Australia though. Maroochy feels the pain sometimes, and the suffering of her people, but there's a strong belief this Cherbourg woman has about this country. The love Maroochy has experienced from non-Aboriginal people gives her some optimism for the future: "I believe love conquers all. I love people no matter what colour they are. I don't think hate or anger corrects anything, it turns a lot of people off."

When Yvette Isaacs became Maroochy Barambah in 1982, not too many folk took much notice. She went on stage, appeared in the film *The Flying Doctors*, and did a smattering of everything. Naturally there was always the music. A rock reggae group she fronted left the audience dazed and clamouring for more. Maroochy went through jazz, rock, soul, pop, classical, and traditional with ease. She enrolled at the National Aboriginal and Islander Dance Theatre in Sydney. "I am an Aquarian, and they say Aquarians get a buzz out of learning things, and that gives you an idea of my personality."

But in many ways she still hadn't dusted off some of those early years at Cherbourg. Behind the mask she presented on stage and in front of the camera, was lurking eleven-year-old Yvette Isaacs, still a little bit self-conscious about her place among white people, and unsure in the pursuit of her dream.

Finally her perfect opportunity arrived. *Black River* was a contemporary Australian opera about black deaths in custody. Written by Andrew and Julianne Schultz, and staged by the Sydney Metropolitan Opera Company, it combined drama, dance, opera and Aboriginal politics. Maroochy with a range that led different teachers to describe her voice as contralto and soprano — won the lead role of Miriam. Here was the vehicle she needed. But she had to create something she had not done before: present an operatic voice that had been dormant for twelve years. Nervous expectation and a lot of hard work combined to make history. *Black River*, which premiered in 1989 in Sydney, won the Sounds Australia Music Critics Award for best performance for an Australian opera or music theatre piece.

All Maroochy's apprehensions suddenly galvanised into a more focused outlook. *Black River* was the catalyst. A parade of excellence followed over the next few years. *Bran Nue Dae* thrilled audiences with its genius, with Maroochy once again starring. The "Building Bridges" concert at Bondi in Sydney confirmed her status as one of the best voices, black or white, in this country. Her unparalleled contribution over almost twenty years was acknowledged with the inaugural Aboriginal Arts Board Performing Arts Fellowship for 1991. After *Black River*, Maroochy toured New South Wales schools performing an educational opera called "Beach Dreaming".

Keep on developing as an artist, is her motto. The response to *Black River* made her reassess her operatic potential, and classical music now has the front running. In the meantime she has recorded an album of rock reggae, gospel and traditional Aboriginal music.

Maroochy is a black swan who spread her talents around the world with a scholarship in 1993. The twelve month study-observation tour of the United States, England, France, Germany and Italy was awarded by the Commonwealth Education Department, to enable Maroochy to take master classes under teachers such as Daniel Ferro at the Juilliard School in New York, and Dr Ferenc Hajtas in Germany.

From an eleven-year-old jiving away with her friends on a Queensland Aboriginal settlement, to the stages of the world's opera houses ... how can anyone predict where children will be when they get older, or predict their achievements? Maroochy didn't have the right attitude as far as her career was concerned all those years ago, but now it's different. "I don't want to be an elderly person who looks back on life and says, 'I should've...I could've...but I didn't.' I don't want to be saying that. I want to say to my grandchildren and everyone else, *I did it.*"

After the fire has been put out, Maroochy intends to return to her homeland around Cherbourg to teach the children acting, music, story-telling, dance, or just about life. "Aboriginal people lived in heaven before Europeans came to this country, with their Bibles and everything else. I'd like to touch that unspoilt paradise again one day.

Every day as I become more and more aware of my Aboriginality, there's just so many beautiful things you discover... it's a joyous experience.

"The truth is, I believe that some days when a baby is born, the good Lord might be in such a very good mood that he gives them more than one talent. I believe that I'm one of those babies, given a few extra talents. It's taken me a while to realise this myself, because I came from a background where Aborigines were told they didn't have a place in society. It's taken a while for it to sink in, that you can do whatever you want to do in any society, whatever the colour of your skin. I'm learning about myself all the time. Every day as I become more and more aware of my Aboriginality, there's just so many beautiful things you discover ... it's a joyous experience."

Maroochy Barambah has an overwhelming presence. She

gives brightness to any situation, but there is something more which makes her stand out. A lot of non-Aboriginal Australians wouldn't understand but it's always been there for everyone to enjoy. Hopefully a day will come when its worth is realised. Maroochy has so much of it, as do many other Aboriginal women. You just have to look at their smiling faces, their cheeky grins, or look into their soulful eyes ... it is a personality, a spirit, a precious thing.

Stan Grant

TV PRESENTER-JOURNALIST

"Mum's great memory of me when I was a kid, is that I'd come home from school, and while the others would go out and play footy straight away, I'd read the newspaper. I'd pick it up on the way home from school, come home, read it, do all that sort of thing, and then go and kick the footy around with the others.

"That was from the earliest days, as far back as Mum can remember. There was always that more serious side to me. I was always reading and wanted to know more about things.

"The other day I was reading this history of a particular area in New South Wales, and I came across my great-grandfather's name, Bill Grant. Beside his name were the words 'story teller'. I guess it's rather appropriate that I'm continuing in much the same way."

It's not surprising Stan Grant is now a well known television presenter and journalist who in 1992 fronted the new Channel 7 current affairs program "Real Life". From a very early age he recognised the hardships and sacrifices his parents went through to create the opportunities for him, and for the rest of the family. Stan wanted to give them something in return for everything they gave him.

He was just different from most of the other kids. Not introverted or extroverted to any degree, but there was a maturity and a sense of order about him, that put him apart from all the others. As if he always knew where he was going, even back then as a young boy. It didn't stunt his childhood or stop him from doing all those things with his mates; he still got in trouble from his mother and father; but while his friends could only see what was in front of them, as most kids can, Stan could already look further ahead.

He was born in Griffith in New South Wales, and is part of the Wiradjuri people, regarded as one of the biggest tribes in

Television presenter-journalist Stan Grant on the set of "Real Life"

eastern Australia. The whole family moved around quite a bit, mainly because his father, Stan, was a labourer and sawmill hand who chased the work. Stan Grant senior didn't have much of an education, but worked long and hard so his children could get the things he and his wife Betty never had when they were younger. Both parents grew up around the Griffith area, and in their day it was a life of tin humpies, dirt floors, and usually only the one bed for all the kids in the family. They were determined to give their own children at least a better start. Stan grew up pretty quickly, having to fend for himself so often, moving to different schools, and adjusting to new people and circumstances. The Grants, like other Aboriginal families, were resilient under the most trying conditions, and it was that resourcefulness which got them through…the capacity to support, share and give.

You had to have all of that, when you lived for a year in a caravan made for two, and there were six in the family. Mum, Dad, and the four kids ate, cooked, did their homework, and slept in this tiny home, Stan's sister sleeping on a fold-out table for most of that time. They couldn't afford a football, so they had to make do with rolled up socks in the backyard.

No matter what level of success you do have, you know where you've come from.

Another time, the family had to chase emus out of a house, before they could move in. No new cars, or any big holidays, or new clothes…a tight budget for a family who scraped by, but who always opened the door to other people. Like Stan's grandfather, or cousins, and aunties and uncles…my home, my food, my bed is yours, and vice versa. Tough days, but very special memories for Stan, and ones he wouldn't exchange for anything. "That stays with you forever. It shapes you. It never leaves you. It breeds a lot of humility into you. So no matter what level of success you do have, and no matter what you might achieve in life, you know there is another side to it. You know where you've come from. And you know the need to be humble about what you have."

> *One of the biggest problems for Aborigines growing up in rural areas is that you don't see the potential of getting an education.*

Things started to look up a bit for the family in the late 1970s when Stan was about fifteen. His parents saved enough money to buy a house in Canberra. "I think the move to Canberra was one of the most important things, because it gave me an opportunity to continue with my education. One of the biggest problems for Aborigines growing up in rural areas is that you don't see the potential of getting an education, because the role models aren't there, and sometimes you're not encouraged to think beyond the town you're in. Moving to Canberra allowed me to see that other world."

Then and there he decided to go for it! To get himself the best schooling he could. If he was going to reach that goal of becoming a journalist, then senior level at high school, and a university degree were almost compulsory. It was the first time he'd actually gone to a major city to live, and to study. Ahead of him were some interesting confrontations, particularly over his Aboriginality.

Stan had no problem whatsoever with being an Aborigine. He was proud of it. What was the big deal? He was part of an exclusive club, and his parents, and their parents before them, were strong people entrenched in the Aboriginal lifestyle and beliefs. He was born of the Wiradjuri, and nothing could be stronger. Why would he even have to think about justifying his colour? However Stan found resistance for the first time in his life at high school.

"I remember giving a speech to my English class. I chose a selection of poems by Kevin Gilbert, one of my relatives. I read these poems, and gave a speech, and spoke about my family. The teacher thought it was terrific. It just didn't occur to me there was anything wrong with it at all. But the backlash I got from a lot of those kids was terrible. They had this stereotypical view, these negative images of Aborigines being drunk and lazy. They could identify an Aborigine who fitted that mould. And because I didn't, it was very confusing for them. I encountered such ignorance quite a bit. I think racism is a word that's so overly used! Sure there is a racist element in Australian society, but a lot of it is bred out of ignorance, simply not knowing what Aborigines are, and who they are. And that's slowly changing, thankfully."

He is what he is! And can never be something else. Even back then Stan was turning all those misjudgments upside down with a positive attitude about himself, and in the process was giving his classmates a thing or two to think about. Most of those other kids remained friends with Stan, but a lot of them just had no idea how to handle it, or how to accept it. More than anything the experience challenged their own values, and they were too young to cope with it. They became frightened because they didn't understand. Stan on the other hand was walking a straight line. He was not going to be pigeon-holed or stereotyped.

Being Aboriginal was something to inspire him, and he found that the best way to influence people was to do your best.

Being Aboriginal was something to inspire him, and he found that the best way to influence people was to do your best. After finishing his senior in Canberra, Stan began a Bachelor of Arts degree at the University of New South Wales in Sydney, majoring in history and politics. He applied for almost every journalism cadetship he possibly could, and in 1983 joined the Macquarie radio network when he was only nineteen years old.

They were great days. Stan did everything from washing the manager's car to reading the news bulletins on air. For Stan it was perfect, although a little daunting. The shaking of the hand-held microphone in his first interview...the slightly nervous quiver in the voice when he read the news live to air. This was for him. There was nothing else in the world he wanted to do. Stan hadn't missed out on anything in life so far, but he and his mum must have known this was what he was all about, why he was reading those newspapers.

The radio station was mayhem most of the time. Having to work to strict deadlines quickly taught him the business of the media: on-the-hour bulletins, with interviews, editing, voice reports. He had to be quick, accurate, and polished as well. The management thought he was all those things and more, because after only seven months at Macquarie, Stan was graded as a D-grade journalist. Over the next four years, he progressed to A-grade.

The time will come when we'll have an Aborigine on the High Court. We'll have Aboriginal QCs, Aboriginal surgeons, people who are just professionals doing a job.

Going from sports to politics, to social issues, to rural problems, was the great benefit of learning his craft at Macquarie. At twenty-three he was well respected for his work, and well liked. He'd achieved a lot for himself, but he also broke through many boundaries for Aboriginal people, by succeeding in his own right in such a competitive market place. "The time will come when we'll have an Aborigine on the High Court. We'll have Aboriginal QCs, Aboriginal surgeons, people who are just professionals doing a job, who happen to be Aborigines, respected for what they do. The recognition will come later."

Accepting a place in mainstream society is one of his strongest wishes, and one he hopes more Aborigines will consider. As he sees it, blame rests on both sides. "White Australia must throw their hands up and say, 'What more do we have to do for these people?' And then they get blamed by some Aborigines for helping to create the social problems. And they say, 'Hang on, I've been paying my taxes, millions of dollars have gone to this, and nothing has changed. Why is that? And you come and blame me again!' And you can understand their resentment.

You can still be your own person and succeed in another world, and be tied spiritually to your own tribal area. You can achieve something in your own right.

"The government and Aborigines themselves should be encouraging individuality and brilliance, to reach out to a world beyond their own little community. I see that as something that hasn't been encouraged too much in the past. You can have the communities. But you can still be your own person and succeed in another world, and be tied spiritually to your own tribal area. Ostracising black kids because they do have ambitions outside their region isn't a healthy thing to do. You know, it's that tall poppy thing in the black community, which isn't nice. I won't accept it at all. I don't know why it happens. Maybe when one person makes it, it scares the others into having to succeed as well! And maybe they're afraid of that and the outcome. So maybe they just refuse to take on the challenge.

"I'm not saying all Aborigines should go out and be great achievers, because obviously everyone can't do that. Just get on with life though, and provide an example to others that you can achieve something in your own right."

For him, it's a big wide world, full of hopes, and gambles. Some pay off, and some don't, but you have to give it a shot! "I believe we should be getting more into step with this country, and becoming a part of it. But we've got an especially strong responsibility because as Aborigines we've been underprivileged. We haven't had the opportunities. When they come, make the most of it, and provide that example to kids, so that they know those opportunities are there for them as well. The rest of society can see what you're doing, and will respect that. So don't make a negative example."

Make no mistake, Stan can see Aborigines being left behind, and he's afraid of that. He wants them to think of the bigger

Stan Grant with wife Karla and daughter Lowanna in Sydney

picture, where they have a responsibility not only to themselves but to all of Aboriginal Australia to move way above where they are now. And showing a positive sign for the others is the way to begin. Not to be frightened of any sort of challenge.

It was the challenge of something new that took Stan to the ABC in 1987, to try his hand at another aspect of the media. Television was too irresistible, with its high profile and glossy image. When he joined as a news reporter in Sydney. Stan was one of the first Aborigines working as a journalist in television around Australia. The ABC in particular employed Aborigines in television and radio, a result of their positive discrimination policy. But Stan wasn't taken on as an Aboriginal trainee. He was an A-grade journalist.

Stan was then transferred to the inferno of Canberra, to work as a political reporter in the ABC bureau. When he was with Macquarie radio, he had covered politics, but certainly not at such an intimate level as he would for the ABC. He was thrown in the deep end, to sink or swim in the murky political waters of Canberra. Stan now regards it as his best time, because it's when he really blossomed professionally. He covered two federal elections every day from beginning to end, about six weeks each.

In 1991, after four years in radio, and four years in television he was lured away from the ABC by commercial television, with the prospect of reaching more people, and perhaps influencing more of the public.

The Channel 7 network approached Stan to present and report for a new prime time current affairs program. It was a courageous move for a few reasons. Firstly, a lot of the experts said another current affairs show at half past six would be an instant failure. And secondly, having an Aboriginal presenter was heading into uncharted territory.

Gerald Stone, the man behind "Real Life", was best known for masterminding "Sixty Minutes" and its runaway success in the early 1980s. Here he was back in town again, after a few years in the States, and at the top of his hit list was Stan Grant and "Real Life". "Gerald and the network had faith in me right from the start. The support by both black and white has been fantastic. I made the point very early on that I didn't only want to be judged as an Aborigine. I wanted to be judged as a journalist, and as a television presenter, and people have judged me by that criteria. Also the press have been good as well. It's just long overdue for Aborigines.

Aborigines are quite capable of achievements in their own right as individuals in mainstream society.

"I'm very pleased and proud to be recognised as a professional, measured by his merits, and also as a role model for other Aborigines, an example to the rest of Australia that Aborigines are quite capable of achievements in their own right as individuals in mainstream society."

Who would ever have imagined that an Aborigine would be fronting a national prime time program on commercial television, five nights a week. Stan Grant changed the face of Australian television forever when he made his first appearance early in 1992. "Real Life" rated very well in some capital cities, and returned in 1993. And if Stan has his way it has ushered in a whole new era for the industry. It must be a wonderful feeling for his own people all over Australia to tune in, and see one of their own presenting a national show, and doing it with so much style.

What do you do when everyone out there is watching your every move? When the success or failure of a new program rests with you...and a lot of money and time has been invested? When you know that your performance will prove that Aborigines are just as good, maybe even better than their non-Aboriginal counterparts? An incredible responsibility for one so young. Stan, in his late twenties, was one of the youngest presenters since Mike Willesee made his debut back in the early seventies.

But there is another side to all of this that disappoints Stan. He can see that Aborigines are treated more seriously from a political perspective: the Coronation Hill decision, and the Eddie Mabo verdict are examples of that. But the portrayal of Aborigines in the media still has major deficiencies. As an Aborigine and a journalist, Stan is frustrated by the constant battle to air Aboriginal items on commercial television. A story Stan did on alcohol and violence in the Aboriginal community of Aurukun is a classic case in point, where it didn't rate at all. Viewers don't want to see stories like that while they're eating their dinner...they'll switch over to brighter news. "Aborigines hardly rate. Like the Muslims ... it's just an instant turn-off factor," Stan said. It's a hard editorial dilemma, balancing what's best for the show when ratings mean so much, and yet addressing significant social issues which affect all Australia. "Gossip and trivia play an important part in any society, but so does the relaying of important substantive views. As a journalist I hope we can always keep sight of that responsibility, by not getting bogged down in the trivial aspects of the lives of people like the royal family. Where do we draw the line between just dishing it up because the public want to hear it, or giving them something that doesn't appeal straight away, but is important knowledge? It's a very fine line, and it's a challenge to keep sight of those responsibilities.

"Ignorance plays such a big role, and that still annoys me. There is so much ignorance out there, and the media hasn't been able to turn that around. It is happening but slowly."

Stan still has great faith in Australia and its people. What exasperates him is that he can see the capacity for a great healing between the races, and a genuine sense of going forward as a people, but all too often self-interests and sheer stubbornness cause the process to jackknife. From the practical vantage point where he sits, he sees major flaws on both sides. The status of Aborigines in their own country has to be raised, and while Aborigines themselves must redress that, non-Aboriginal Australia needs to accord Aborigines a much higher level of respect. Justice, in a way, for the treatments of a yesterday.

"In theory I can see the benefit of a treaty, and the justice of according Aborigines more respect. But I think you have to be pragmatic. I can't see it happening. If you talk about a treaty, you're going to alienate a lot of people, for what result? Is it going to change anything?" Stan can't see how a treaty will solve the appalling infant mortality rate, the high imprisonment rate, the high unemployment, and the tragic health conditions of some Aboriginal communities. From what he's observed, the treaty push and the land rights scenario simply haven't been the answer for Aboriginal people across Australia. It doesn't add up! According to Stan, if they've won some land rights battles over the last twenty years or so, and a whole Aboriginal industry has developed as a result of millions of dollars of government funding in all sectors, then why are Aborigines still on the bottom of the pile? He would love the answer to that. For Stan, those things clearly haven't worked, and it begs the questions, what are the aims here? and where are Aboriginal people going?

I still haven't lost my land. It's still there to me! The land my father and my grandfather were born on.

"When I was a kid, my grandfather used to say to me, you don't look at what you've lost, you look at what you've got. I still haven't lost my land. It's still there to me! The land my father and my grandfather were born on. If they can convince me that sovereignty and being a separate nation is going to be a benefit for Aborigines, then fine, I'm all for it. But I haven't been convinced. How does it work with two-and-a-half percent of a population of a country? It's about time white Australia realised we deserve a share of this country, and deserve respect. And it's about time black Australia realised we'd better make the most of our opportunities! We're going in circles, and until we know what we want, I just don't see where we're heading. It's frustrating. We have got so much to offer this country, rather than to sit around and let it fritter away."

For Stan, being an Aborigine is a strong sense of belonging to this country. It's a real deep sense of belonging to the land. Knowing your family and that there is something more than the last two hundred years.

He admits to being demanding of himself, and others, a bit of a perfectionist who won't suffer fools, and wants people to at least do their best.

Stan has resigned himself to being public property, but keeps his family — wife Karla and young daughter Lowanna — away from all the attention. Stan has never been a great "people" person, preferring a small quiet gathering of friends rather than gala social events. But as a television anchor man he has been called upon quite a lot for publicity and promotional work. It's not the most favoured part of the job, but he understands how vital it is. One day he would like to work overseas, and with Aboriginal media groups. Acting and writing are other possibilities.

Underneath the television image dwells an artist of diverse persuasions. One day when you least expect it, Stan Grant may strap on the trusty old guitar, and rock the foundations of your nearest concert hall! A bit of blues, a bit of country, and some real stuff from the heart...the riffs were pretty hot back in the early days when he was a teenager with the band.

Linda Bonson rehearsing at the dance school, Adelaide University

Linda Bonson

DANCER

"When I found out I was accepted to an Aboriginal dance school in Sydney, I had a dream. I dreamt I saw a man dancing with a snake. He had this snake wrapped all around his body, and he had just a loincloth on. It was in a room, and it was cloudy and overcast, so there were no shadows anywhere. There was a little grandstand of people in the room, and they were watching this man from India perform. He was dancing with this snake. And he came up to me. He saw me, and came up to me. He put the snake in front of me — in my face. Sort of like saying, touch it! Touch it! I touched it with my finger, fighting all my fear. Just with my finger. And then the dream ended. I guess what it meant to me was, go for it! Go and learn to dance, because there are great things to be discovered from it. Don't be scared."

Linda Bonson — whose tribal totems are the King Brown snake and the brolga — had that dream eleven years ago, and to this day she remembers it. Back then when she was nineteen years old, it was a sign of what lay ahead, of the exciting challenge of dance. Now though, it serves as a reminder of lost days and opportunities, of a whole slab of her life gone, never to return.

This is the story of a woman who overcame a most shattering experience. The world gave her everything, but, just as magically, just as quickly, it was taken away. The dreams of being on stage, and fulfilling those ambitions evaporated, and she took a long time to come to terms with those memories.

Now, Linda has rediscovered that desire. The years have gone by, but the passion for dance and expression has never wilted. It was waiting for a revival of spirit and mind. The energy of the teenage years might not be as strong, but the passion is there, to dance, and dance, and dance.

I suppose she got it from her father, John Bonson. He is an

Aboriginal-Torres Strait Islander. And he loved dancing. It was something that was in him, and Linda has inherited that appreciation and feel for dance. When she was growing up in Darwin, her father used to do the *hula* dance with Linda's aunties at home, or even in some of the clubs around town, and Linda was encouraged to join in. The *hula* was adopted by Torres Strait Islanders from the Polynesians who settled there. Although her parents, John and Patricia, divorced when she was very young, they both taught her to be happy. "My mum has always told me, it's not the destination that matters, it's the journey."

My mum has always told me, it's not the destination that matters, it's the journey.

And what a journey it was for Linda back then. The thing she remembers so well about her childhood in Darwin is the free and easy lifestyle, playing with all her cousins, and all her friends. The responsibility of raising Linda was left to her father. Her dad wasn't alone though, because with closeknit Aboriginal family ties, all of Linda's uncles, aunties and grandparents made sure he was doing a good job. There wasn't a great need for concern however. Although her main hobby was getting on to the dance floor and learning new numbers, this young lady was levelheaded. At the height of disco fever around the world in the mid to late seventies, if you wanted to catch up with Linda and her gathering, then it was simply a case of door knocking from one nightclub to the other in Darwin.

She wasn't there for anything else but the chance to dance, coming home in the early hours of the morning with sore feet. But it wasn't only the latest contemporary music which had all her attention. There was the rhythm and mystery of Aboriginal and Torres Strait Islander dancing, which was so much a vital influence on her.

Her tribal ancestors from Ngkurr on the Roper River and Lake Nash in the Northern Territory danced under the stars for centuries, telling the stories of life, and their Dreamtime. The stomping of the feet on the dusty ground was powerful, a hypnotic celebration of their culture. The singing and the clap sticks rang out for miles and miles. If you heard it, you couldn't help but become a part of it.

Linda's great-grandmother played a strong part in those rituals. Dolly Bonson became a legend of that country. Early this century she was taken, as a child, from the banks of the Roper River by a white woman. The two of them became very close friends, and learnt from each other. Dolly was known as "Bett Bett the little Black Princess", and was portrayed by Jeannie Gunn in her book *We of the Never Never*, which was released as a film in 1982. Dolly passed away a few years ago at the age of ninety-six, but her spirit is still alive, and continues from one generation to the next. The links of such heritage can never be severed.

Her spirituality, which had teased and tempted her for years, was now out in the open.

Linda left school at the age of sixteen when study became a little boring. A while later she was in Adelaide staying with relatives, when her mother passed through on the way to Tasmania and Linda joined her. Then an Aboriginal woman told her about an Aboriginal and Islander dance school in Sydney. She knew this was for her, but first of all there was an audition to get through. Hundreds of hopefuls from all around Australia turned up for the week-long try-out, and Linda was accepted as a student for a five-year intensive course in dance, acting, and singing. She was now nineteen years old and ready to take on the whole world. Her spirituality, which had teased and tempted her for years, was now out in the open: Linda wanted to get cracking and learn about these cultural dances and their powers. She had no strong ambitions to become the greatest, she was just a young lady experiencing something new and exciting, and was taking it day by day.

Those days were very special to her. "Something felt right about it. It's a spiritual thing. You can't put your finger on it. It's like a hunch! Like a sixth sense." Life seemed perfect. However, after only eighteen months Linda and the school parted company after a disagreement that couldn't be resolved. She left Sydney devastated, and went to live in Adelaide. She tried to get the school out of her mind, but it haunted her. One minute she was in the middle of her fantasy, with the magic of her dance around her, the next she was on the outside. It was like her life support system had been turned off. "I was really cut up about it for years. It seemed to me that Sydney, and Aboriginal dance was my little niche in life. It was there, not here in Adelaide. Like, what am I doing here for God's sake. What happened! I felt bitter and angry about a lot of things. I really had the world in the palm of my hand. So many opportunities to do whatever I wanted to do! It was all there for the taking."

Linda just couldn't shut out dance, the energy of it was too overwhelming

---

Linda tried her hand at acting, but didn't take to it. Modelling was something she really did enjoy, but it didn't grab her as a full time career. Linda just couldn't shut out dance, the energy of it was too overwhelming. She wanted to be happy again, to find that missing piece of her life. At last she understood she could never get those years back, but her life hadn't ended, there were still so many wonderful things to do. There was a yearning inside, something telling her that dance was what she had to do. Not what she chose to do, but what she had to do. Linda was following her heart. That's what was leading her.

It was the physical satisfaction of dancing. It was the only way of expressing herself, and it was also spiritually fulfilling.

A friend persuaded her to apply to the University of Adelaide to do a Bachelor of Arts in dance. In 1991 she auditioned and was accepted. At the age of twenty-eight Linda was on track again … back to her first love! All she wanted to do was take off her shoes, and spend all day dancing as if she was back in Darwin. But there were essays, and exams, and tutorials, and a whole lot of study.

Despite the heartache of the previous eight years, she was now

Dancer Linda Bonson

ready to have another go. "There's no Aboriginal music or dance in this course I'm doing. There's a lot of studying and even tutors as well to help me, things like that, that I've never done before. A friend said to me, well, if you're dancing you should be happy, doesn't matter where you are. I thought about that for a while. But I'm only just beginning to let go of the past. I want to make it happen now. I couldn't make it happen before. Now I want to give it a go again."

Though there is no traditional element within the course, it does take a holistic approach, which involves yoga. The combination of yoga and dance has taught her so much about her body, and how to breathe properly. Good breath control is very important in yoga and also in dance. The course combines the academic with the practical, including classical ballet, modern dance, Flamenco, Balinese dance, improvisation, performance production, choreography and costume. But to her nothing compares to the exhilaration of traditional dance.

If only the non-Aboriginal students in her class could at least get a bit of that sensation. She is the first Aborigine registered for this course at Adelaide University. Few Aboriginal men or women have studied this art form.

She has performed Aboriginal and Islander dance with a fringe festival group from the Adelaide Hills, and not too long ago a visiting traditional troupe from Sydney enticed her on stage to participate in some Mornington Island dancing. Wow! That's what she really loves to do. Linda got painted up and joined in.

It's like a big wave we're on at the moment, with all this Aboriginal art, music, and culture sweeping Australia. Nothing can stop it.

Every time she sees her friends from some of those dance groups up on stage, it makes her extremely proud, and brings her to tears of happiness. "It does hurt me in a way though when I see those dancers, because I know you can't go back in time, you have to only go forward. But they do make me happy. They're positive people. They're creative people. They're my kind of people. It's like a big wave we're on at the moment, with all this Aboriginal art, music, and culture sweeping Australia. Nothing can stop it."

Her courage is quite amazing. At a time when most people are well and truly into their careers in dance, and some have given it away after all the years of stress on the body, here is Linda Bonson determined to start again, and do something with her talents. Dancing is her priority at the moment, but eventually she'd love to create her own performance. One of her main goals is to write, direct, choreograph and perform in her own Aboriginal dance. Let the sounds of the clap sticks, and the didgeridoo, and the singing mesmerise the audience. For Linda it's a feeling that is hard to explain. It simply takes over her emotions, when she hears those sounds. Often a contemporary rock and roll song on the radio will inspire her to get up and dance. Traditional music gives her a feeling just as good, but in a different way.

"If you want to think of an almighty presence that is everywhere, is in everything, and in everyone, then it is the Aboriginal culture. Our ancestors, our Dreamtime! When I've danced traditional dance, you could just feel the power. And when you're in a group, you combine with everyone else, like you are attracting the ancestors. It brings them to us."

All her life she's remembered what her parents taught her as a child: to try and be happy, and treat everyone with respect, just as she would expect to be treated. Her integrated upbringing in Darwin has served her well, but there have been those times where she's been left wondering about people. One such incident occurred at Rottnest Island off Perth in Western Australia, when she was about fifteen. She and her mother walked into a restaurant on the island. They passed a table of businessmen, and Linda heard one of them say: "Bloody Asians, they should go back to their own country." It upset her, but she could laugh about it later, because they couldn't even get the nationality right. "Racism is horrible. You see it everywhere, in people's faces, it's in the vibrations they give off to you. It's on TV, it's in advertising, it's on billboards, it's everywhere. It's there when you hop on to a bus. It makes me think of the devil! It's evil! That's what I think of straight away. I think the devil lives in that person. That's how

I feel. Because I'm a sensitive person to things like that. If I feel racism around me, I think, now I'm in the company of the devil."

Incidents like that haven't made her bitter about her country. Linda Bonson has proclaimed her Aboriginality and the love of dance. And that's enough for her. As long as she can go back to her country, Ngkurr, now and again, to reinforce her Aboriginality and respond to her traditional cravings. It's been a long time since she's walked that earth. She can do the *leaf* and the *water* dance from her tribal area. These dances describe the nature of movement: for the *leaf* dance Linda holds two small leafy branches and swishes them together. Both dances are often performed with the rhythm of clap sticks and a didgeridoo, the feet lifting up quickly in time to the music. But Linda wants to learn more, and perhaps the inspiration for her own dance choreography is waiting there for her. Who knows where it will lead. Like her mother says, it's not the destination but the journey.

Archie Roach

SINGER-SONGWRITER

There's something everyone should know, and that is you can't have one without the other. They go hand in hand in everything they do and in just about everything they expect out of life. Alongside Archie Roach is his best friend, his wife, his companion Ruby Hunter. They've tasted the good times, and looked out at the world through the dim outline of bottles. Few can possibly imagine what it was like. Almost every day of those years was simply a struggle for themselves and their family, and for the money to satisfy their need.

Can you get so low where nothing really matters except the booze? Where every day is lost into another? Drunkenness, fights...the jungle of the underground ... both Archie and Ruby have now stepped out of that darkness, and thousands out there are grateful. Archie's music has sent out a message already, but it's only just begun...if you close your eyes, and listen very carefully to the music and the lyrics, it'll bring you much closer to what this man and this woman have experienced, and what they're trying to say.

I'm one of the lucky ones. I grabbed a piece of their magic on Yarrabah Aboriginal reserve outside of Cairns. Archie and Ruby got up in front of thirty or so people in a basketball shed late on a Friday night, and blew us away with their honesty. I will never forget Archie and Ruby.

No matter where he is and who is there, be it Melbourne's Myer Music Bowl in front of thousands of people, or simply a small gathering of Aboriginal people in the middle of nowhere, Archie will deliver to you a truth and gentleness...because he doesn't know any other way. Certainly if anyone had reason to be bitter at the world for what it did to him, it would have to be Archie.

It was the late 1950s, he was a child enjoying his life with his

Together: Ruby Hunter and Archie Roach

family in the Kirrae Wurrong tribal region in Framingham, Victoria. There was so much ahead, the richness of Aboriginal culture, the family unity, learning the tribal language. However, other people had different ideas. Before Archie could even get started on that wonderful journey, children's welfare officials stepped in and changed his direction forever.

They saw the small humpies pieced together with corrugated iron, the dirt floors, the lack of electricity, and they mistook this for negligence.

While his parents were away up the road, the department officers took Archie and two of his sisters. It was based on a misunderstanding white people had back then of Aboriginal life. They saw the small humpies pieced together with corrugated iron, the dirt floors, the lack of electricity, and they mistook this for negligence. They simply compared it to their own European style of life, and decided these Aborigines were mistreating the children. Three children were gathered up in a car, and driven away as though nothing unusual was happening. Three-year-old Archie just sat in the car wondering who these people were, and where he was going. He couldn't quite remember seeing them around the area before. But there was nothing to worry about. *Mum and Dad wouldn't let me and my sisters go with these people for a holiday if they weren't nice people.* As his little face peered back at the camp through the rear window, he wasn't to know he would never see his mother and father again.

It was called assimilation. For the betterment of Aboriginal people. The authorities said it was all for the good of the children, despite the fact they'd just torn a family right down the middle. Archie and his two sisters, Myrtle and Alma, were put in an institution in a Melbourne suburb, with the hope they'd one day find a nice caring white family and be fostered out or maybe adopted. This was thought to be the only way they'd get the right education, and become valuable members of society. Archie's other brothers and sisters were also taken away.

Because he'd been taken at an early age, Archie had only a

jumbled recollection of his parents. This was now his life: white schools, with white friends, and no contact with his family or Aboriginal teachings. Over the years Archie became a bit of a failure as a foster child. Every time he was sent to a foster family for a week-end, he would play up, and come back with instructions never to return.

But eventually in the mid-sixties there was someone who took to him, and vice versa. The Cox's were a typical suburban Melbourne family with nothing much special to offer except understanding and love. It was good enough for Archie Roach, however, and he moved in with them, and became one of the family. He got on well with their daughter Mary, and Mrs Cox in particular seemed to understand Archie more than anyone else. She introduced him to cups of tea, and every afternoon they would just sit down and talk about everything and nothing at all.

How come your parents are white?

But it was only a matter of time before something set it all in motion. He knew he was a different colour to most of the other children at school, but what that represented was a mystery. At the age of eleven, a friend provided that little spark, which started Archie thinking about himself and his heritage. While walking his mate home one afternoon, his friend turned to him and said, "How come your parents are white?" An innocent enough question, but one Archie couldn't answer. Up until then he hadn't thought about it, because he'd often seen other dark kids with white families and simply assumed it was normal. No one had told him anything about his real family, and where he came from and who he was. The Cox's told him he was Aborigine, but they couldn't tell him anything else, because they didn't know anything themselves. Questions swirled around inside his head. Over the next couple of years he learnt a bit about Aboriginal culture from books, and from what his foster family could tell him.

It wasn't until almost 1970, when Archie was about fourteen, that the one vital piece of information linking his past to the present was sent to him. His sister Myrtle wrote telling him their mother had passed away. He vaguely remembered Myrtle, but who was his mother? How could he let the tears flow for someone he hadn't even known? The Cox's had no response to the letter.

"I took their silence for guilt. I was thinking they knew all along, and they wouldn't tell me nothing." Archie felt betrayed. He was left floundering in loneliness...if no one was going to tell him the truth, he'd go and find it himself. Archie left and became a bit like a fugitive on the run. He was still a ward of the state, but his objective now was to piece together this jigsaw puzzle that the government had created. He couldn't understand how people could be so cruel, treating Aborigines with contempt.

In the space of a year or so, Archie Roach changed from being a suburban North Strathmore teenager to a young man fighting for survival on the streets of Melbourne. He quickly learnt to be street-smart, never to use his real name, and how to avoid the police. Along the way he found out that Myrtle was in Sydney. This was the chance to sort out the crazy nightmare. Archie arrived in Sydney, but soon found out his sister had returned to Melbourne. It seemed whenever he came close to the answer, something would put up a barricade to block him.

With hardly any money left, and nowhere to go, he settled in Sydney for a while. It was different from Melbourne, but who cares! As long as it's got the "hungry mile" — the place in every capital city in Australia where desperates can get a feed, a bed, a hand-out, and most importantly, a drink. It didn't take him long to slide right in there, and pretty soon he was one of the familiar faces around the streets.

She hit me fair in the mouth and started crying!
She said I'm ya sister Dianne.

One night, however, something extraordinary happened to Archie. He had run into this lady quite a number of times on the street. They shared conversation and drink now and again, but there was no reason to take any special notice of her.

This night they were all sitting around sharing a few bottles, when Archie blurted out his real name. "This lady came over, and started talking to me and she said, 'What did ya say ya name was?' I said, Archie Roach. She started asking me all these questions about my brothers and sisters, and of me mother and father. I told her what I knew. And when she was finally satisfied that I was telling the bloody truth, that I was who I said I was, she knocked me off me chair! She hit me fair in the mouth! I'm trying to get away from this lady. What's wrong with this woman? She then grabbed me and started crying! She said 'I'm ya sister Dianne.' She was one of my sisters, and we didn't know, after seeing each other almost every day."

His tears could at last be shared with one of his own. They spoke about their lives and their family. He learnt that there had been five sisters and three brothers in the Roach family. Archie never got a chance to know his mother or father, before they passed away. Just once he would have loved to have sat down with both of them, if only to look into their eyes for a moment. The more he thought about his situation, the more confused and angry he became. And then he thought about those government people. How the hell would *they* like it, if *they* were taken away from their natural parents, and never told a damn thing! When he felt like that he drank harder to try and get rid of the aching in his heart.

Dianne described their parents, Nellie and Archie. Both were admired by many people, black and white. Archie senior was a real gentleman, and well respected throughout the region for his kindness. When you sit down and talk to Archie, it's very easy to understand that about his father, because his son is exactly the same.

The jigsaw puzzle would never be complete. The missing pieces were his mum and dad, but at least he'd found out about his family, and also about his culture. Archie returned to Melbourne, and took up with a young Aboriginal girl from Adelaide, with a similar history. Ruby Hunter and Archie Roach were teenage lovers on the streets of Melbourne. They rolled from day to day without any real purpose, except to get high on a few bottles of whatever they could find. They fought alongside each other — against other drunks and against the police — and they drank together.

You couldn't mistake the passion of these two young people.

It was not a common courtship, but you couldn't mistake the passion of these two young people who had found contentment in each other's company. It was a hazy coexistence, where many nights were spent sleeping out in freezing cold weather, and if you managed to get a feed you were doing all right. Most times though, all of the money was spent over the counter of hotel bars or bottle shops.

It was a real lottery if they woke up between warm sheets at a boarding house. They had to think more about that over the years, because Ruby and Archie were now parents with two little boys to look after. Regardless of their alcoholism, both were aware of what they'd suffered when they lost their families, and they had a steely determination the same thing would not happen to their children. But this horrible addiction had really got a hold of both of them, and was slowly draining them of everything. Archie was the one who seemed most affected. His mind, body, and spirit were eroding at a rapid rate with all this self-abuse. He'd lost touch with himself completely, and was beginning to mistreat Ruby and the children.

One afternoon, Ruby decided to change: "What really woke me up, was when I was about twenty-seven years old. I was lining up my children on the soup van. It was where we'd go for a feed. Amos and Eban, they were about two and three. And it really touched me when I saw my kids lined up with me. That was the realisation then! We ended up back in the park at Fitzroy that day. That was the day I walked away from Archie. I grabbed the kids and said 'See ya later'." That was the last time Ruby Hunter touched any alcohol. They say that Aboriginal women are the backbone of the family, well Ruby was about to prove that correct.

Ruby and the kids went to a rehabilitation halfway house for women, and Archie spent three weeks in hospital, after collapsing unconscious with an epileptic fit. After almost a decade of living like this, Archie had finally reached the crossroads. So began his and Ruby's climb out of purgatory to a brand new world, one they knew was there, but had always appeared way out of focus. It was one of the toughest periods in Archie's life. If he ever wanted Ruby and the boys back, then alcohol couldn't be a part of the family any more.

Getting started on the booze was easy compared with the mental and physical anguish they both had to go through to cleanse themselves completely. They sought professional help at rehabilitation centres in Melbourne. One of the real difficulties for Archie was doing it without the guiding presence of his friend. However that's what Ruby wanted. She kept an eye on him through her circle of friends but made sure he was doing it all by himself.

After six months Ruby and the boys moved into a flat at St Kilda, right next door to a bottle shop. It wasn't a deliberate plot by her, it was a case of simple economics...a nice clean flat, and the price was right. The invitation was sent to Archie. Two lost souls who found each other on the streets many many years ago, and had lost it all in pain and sorrow, were now about to take a second shot at life.

Temptations were around them all the time, but they had each other now, and they grew stronger and stronger. Archie and Ruby became such fine examples, they worked as alcohol counsellors travelling through country Victoria. There was still a way to go, but now they had a direction.

One thing they'd always had was music. Even when Archie was whacked out on grog, the old guitar was always by his side. A few years earlier, Archie had taken a day off the drink to collect a prestigious singer-songwriter award at the 1978 National Aboriginal Country Music Awards in Adelaide.

He began singing in a coffee lounge in St Kilda. It was a place for ex-drunks and whoever to meet for company and encouragement every Saturday night. For a bit of entertainment Archie was persuaded — or more like dobbed-in — by his mates to strum a few chords for the patrons. Those friends of his knew talent when they heard it. Eventually Archie overcame his nerves, and gave those fortunate people the first taste of his musical and songwriting ability.

From there he built up a following in Melbourne, with guest appearances at multicultural events, and as a back-up for other artists. It was a productive time in Archie's life. Ruby, himself, and the boys were together as a family and happy, and all of those past memories were a fountain of inspiration for Archie's musical career.

The radio station switchboard lit up. Everyone wanted to know who this Archie Roach was.

The next step up came at a public radio station when Archie was interviewed about one of his own songs, "Took the Children Away", and the history behind it. After talking about his life, Archie sat down and moved everyone with his poignant song. He didn't have to search very far to find a meaning to the lyrics. All he had to do was play the opening chords, and he was transported back to those years at the camp with his family...it all just came pouring out of him. The station switchboard lit up. Everyone wanted to know who this Archie Roach was.

He was now well and truly on his way. Countless interviews and television appearances followed. Paul Kelly, a leading singer-songwriter, invited Archie to be part of a line-up of Australian musicians at a big concert in Melbourne.

"That's when everything turned around for me. I was approached to do a record in 1989. Paul Kelly came around, and we sang a few songs to him, and he chose a lot of the material that went on *Charcoal Lane*".

Paul Kelly and Steve Connolly co-produced and played on *Charcoal Lane*, Archie's debut album, which was written by Archie and Ruby. Critically it was hailed around Australia. It won the ARIA Award for "indigenous album of the year" in

Archie Roach and his foster son Terrence in the backyard of their Melbourne home

1990. Archie was presented with the award in 1991, and won the ARIA Award for "best new talent" that same year. His song "Took the Children Away" in 1991 won the Inaugural Human Rights Songwriting Award, and in 1992 Archie was named Folk Performer of the Year at the Mo Entertainment Awards in Sydney.

Archie was performing at a concert when another piece of the jigsaw puzzle was put in place. "I was just about to walk off stage and this lady came running up to me. She had a big envelope and said 'There's some photos of you when you were a child, and a letter explaining things!' I couldn't work out who she was for a while until I looked at her real hard. She'd gotten a bit older, but it was Mary, Mary Cox. And she sat down beside me and started crying. She said she was so sorry for what happened. 'We didn't know anything that was going on with you children.' I said, Mary, it's alright, that was a long time ago."

She said the welfare department had told her parents that Archie was the only survivor of his family, after a fire ripped through their house at Dandenong. The two embraced like long lost friends usually do. They now have a strong brother-sister relationship which hasn't been spoiled by those sad events all those years ago.

Sadly though, the lady he used to enjoy those cups of tea with every afternoon on the patio, passed away shortly after he was reunited with Mary. He hadn't seen Mrs Cox in over twenty years, but at her funeral he paid his final respects, to a woman he loved very much. A simple thing like enjoying a cuppa with Mrs Cox is one part of his memory that hasn't let him down. They are the little things he'll never forget, because it was two people learning from each other with total respect.

Since he gave the bottle away all those years ago, Archie Roach has tracked down his family and keeps in regular contact with them. His brothers and sisters and his uncles and aunties are very much a part of his life. His Uncle Banjo had been abused by the system, but he once told Archie he wasn't angry, that more than anything he felt a deep sadness for those people. A lot of strength has come from Archie's uncles and aunties, who have an enormous amount of spiritual peace about them. There's no use looking for any spitefulness in Archie, because it'd be a futile exercise.

"I've got no animosity. I've got good friends. I love people. It's not really the common person in the street that's really done it to me. And that's what I try and teach my children too. When I sing about the Gubba in a song, it's not about the lad across the road, it's talking about a lad in power.

"Every time I perform, I think about how my life was and what it is now. There are times when I need to stop completely still and take in what's happening at that very moment, pulling yourself up and realising where you are. This is what I was always meant to do.

"A lot of my songs come from the immediate feeling, or something that's been with me for a while, and finally I'm able to get it out through song.

Even now it doesn't matter how many times I sing 'Took the Children Away', it still affects me the same way.

"I usually don't say too much, but when I'm up on stage it's like another world. Even now it doesn't matter how many times I sing 'Took the Children Away', it still affects me the same way, and it's like a new release, like it's still here inside. It'll never leave me. But every time I sing it, I let a fraction of it go. Maybe that's why people have reacted to it the way they have."

Both times I saw Archie and Ruby in concert, in Brisbane, and at Yarrabah Mission outside Cairns, there was no fanfare with either performance. Just a mob of people hanging around and tapping their feet. The more I think about that night at Yarrabah though, the more it makes me smile.

I was driven out by a friend, and was pretty excited, not only about seeing Archie and Ruby again, but also about seeing this reserve for the first time. Unfortunately there'd been some sort of communication breakdown. Archie and Ruby arrived from

Lotus Glen Jail, southwest of Cairns, where they had taken their music to the inmates. No gear had been set up, and there were about a dozen people at the shed, myself included. Because the concert hadn't been publicised, Archie, Ruby and friends wandered down to a packed-out canteen to drum up a bit of an audience, leaving the other support band members to decide whether or not to go ahead at such a late stage. After a long deliberation, they decided to give it a go, regardless of the crowd size. Everything was ready to fire at around ten o'clock. I sat down with a cool drink in the hand, with the thirty or so locals who'd moseyed in for a look see, all prepared for another mesmerising show from Archie and Ruby.

At around half past eleven on a lazy Friday night, they hit the floorboards of that old basketball shed with so much energy, everyone sat hypnotised. Well, most of us anyway. There was a couple of elderly women who had the dancing shoes on. They were great. I don't know what it is, but they always seem to pick me as a dancing partner. What a great evening it turned out to be, despite the early hiccups.

The gutsy power of Ruby's voice stood out. This tiny woman was right alongside her man, sharing the harmonies, as well as showing off her guitar talents, and some of her own songs. They sang some songs from Archie's new album, *Jamu Dreaming*. Not too many people had heard this new material. It was dynamic stuff, a great mixture of ballads and uptempo tunes, and certainly not too much of a political statement.

What I wrote about on Charcoal Lane *I suppose* *was really misunderstood.*

Archie's music deals with Aboriginal issues in this country, and touches on the personal hardships of his and Ruby's life. But he is also very much his own man.

"What I wrote about on *Charcoal Lane* I suppose was really misunderstood. Sure it dealt with a lot of things that affected Aboriginal people, but I am a separate person from my race. What happened to me, and what I wrote about was just about

Archie Roach as a person. Granted an Aboriginal person, but as Archie Roach. So a lot of my songs I write now, I'd rather be seen as a singer-songwriter.

Because you're an Aboriginal person, people think that you must have a statement or an opinion on everything. I think that slowly they're starting to see the music as being just good music.

"Because you're an Aboriginal person, people think that you must have a statement or an opinion on everything. I think that slowly they're starting to see the music as being just good music."

At a concert at a university, Archie stopped in the middle of a song to sort out a disturbance in the audience. Before anything became nasty, he jumped off the stage and had a few words with a young Aborigine, who seemed to be full of hate and anger. After the show, the two of them had a chat. Archie spoke about many things, notably about living together as a united community, not divided by colour, and how vital it was to work and survive together, to guarantee some sort of future.

"If I was talking like that ten, fifteen years ago, I would've thought there was something wrong with me. I did some stupid things, but it wasn't getting me anywhere, it wasn't endearing people to me. I say to those young Aboriginal kids who are angry today, that there are people who don't have a racist outlook on life. There's people who are shamed. Shamed to be white because of what happened in the past! Be proud of yourself, and your people! We can live, and we can contribute to the wider society, but we can still have our own culture! Ya see!"

Exciting things lie ahead for Archie and Ruby. In 1992 they went to Canada and North America and were well received at the famous Vancouver Folk Festival, and at singing engagements in Seattle and San Francisco.

While the attention is flattering for Archie, he wonders why it has been reserved for him, when artists he has admired for years are still battling for some recognition, even though they were the pioneers...it's an unfair balance. Like most singers, Archie would dearly love to make the grade in America, and find a market there for his music, but if it doesn't happen, well too bad. His life revolves around Ruby and the children. In a unanimous show of hands they have voted for their own block of dirt — "Just to have a bit of land where I know this can remain for my children." Archie and Ruby are both deeply connected to the earth, and now more than ever understand what it gives them, what real value it holds for them.

Shirley Nirrpurranydji, Arnhem Land principal, with Sophie Henry

Shirley Nirrpurranydji

SCHOOL PRINCIPAL

There was something about this country! Whenever it was mentioned to me, or whenever I saw pictures of it, it evoked strange sensations — feelings of a real mystery, and a rawness. It tugged away at my own spirituality. It was a time when I didn't understand my heritage, and yet I felt something with these traditional people standing so proud on their land, as if they were looking out over the rest of Australia. I was scared of it, yet always, always in love with it, in some enticing way. I saw it for the first time at about seven or eight years of age. It was one of the first times I'd ventured into the big city, and I was there to see a film about Aborigines on their tribal land. The memory is a little blurred now but I do remember looking up at the big screen, and seeing a world which seemed out of place, and puzzling to me.

Where was it? And who were these people? It didn't make a great deal of sense to me, although it left a haunting image. I never forgot it. In the last few years I've come so close to it, but not quite close enough to enter. I've been on the edge, wondering what it must be like, and hoping my day would come.

Well, finally, the life long mystery was right before my eyes. Here I was deep in the heart of Arnhem Land, and below was some of the most breath-taking country in all Australia. I looked out the window of the small plane, awestruck at what surrounded me, and felt curious and guarded at what this country might offer after so many years of carrying it around in my head. Yeah! I could feel it getting stronger and stronger.

My destination was the Gapuwiyak community in east Arnhem Land, about six hundred kilometres directly east of Darwin, and a couple of hours drive from the coastline. Gapuwiyak means salty water, and most people might not find it appealing, stuck out in the middle of nowhere, with only Lake Evella to look at, and no beach or ocean...just plenty of red dust and the hot sun and a population of about five hundred to keep you company. Not a big attraction for most, but it felt pretty good to me. There was a stunning beauty about Gapuwiyak that I could see straight away. Or perhaps I was a little biased. Coming from a concrete jungle of a million people, this was an oasis in the bush...a sprinkling of houses set along about six streets criss-crossing each other...a shop, a school, a police station, a church, and a community centre...that's about it.

I had waited a lifetime to make it to the promised land.

But by opening the door of the plane, I had entered another world, where I was an outsider, a visitor. In all my experiences and travels in my own country, never had I felt like this before. What a truly unbelievable sensation. It seems I had waited a lifetime to make it to the promised land.

The walk into town wasn't a problem, despite the heat. It was a chance to take my time, and have a good look at the place. Understandably there weren't too many people around in the midday heat, only mad dogs and myself. Everybody else was inside in the air-conditioning, enjoying lunch, and getting ready for the final few hours of work. That's exactly what Shirley Nirrpurranydji was doing. I had travelled 3,000 kilometres to meet Shirley, who at the time was principal-in-training at the Gapuwiyak Community School. So in the meantime I entertained myself with the school children or should I say I became the entertainment for them.

Not too many visitors come in from the city, so when they do, everybody wants to know. When I first sat down in the library, a couple of Aboriginal children came up to say hello. But by the time Shirley arrived twenty minutes later, I was surrounded: the word had spread, they came right in and sat down on the floor next to me. I just sat there for most of the time in the middle of the room, with no idea what they were saying, just nodding my head in agreement now and again, which seemed to make them happy.

Let go of your own world, and let Arnhem Land be the teacher.

Shirley and I got on well straight away. It didn't take too long to work out that if you didn't like Shirley, then you had some real problems. There were so many things which told me a lot about this woman in the few hours we spent together on the first day I was there...from her warmth as a friend, to her charm as a host. Her natural beauty echoed through everything around her. In Shirley I saw this whole country, and the traditions passed down from family to family over thousands of years...and I knew it was with me, right beside me. Everyone should meet a Shirley Nirrpurranydji in their lifetime, or see this country. Remember though to let go of your own world, and let Arnhem Land be the teacher...there is so much to learn and to see.

I sat in the shade of a mango tree with Shirley and some of her family, the school principal Tad Henry, and his three-year-old daughter Sophie.

What a great sight it was when Shirley swept Sophie up in her arms, and proceeded to talk to her in her Aboriginal language as well as in English: to see this tribal woman sitting down on the ground with a white child in her arms, their arms wrapped around one another, exchanging cultures and learning from each other, as well as being simply two good friends. I felt so privileged to be there, and to be a part of it. I couldn't take my eyes off them. In a way I was jealous of this little girl for what she already knew, and for being able to speak the tribal language. Sophie had lived with these people since the day she was born, and was adopted into their ways. She had this wonderful head start on everyone else.

The two of them like that together represented the view Shirley has for the future of Australia. I understood what she was giving to Sophie while they sat under the mango tree. It was something others would never learn in a lifetime. What would this child be like though in fifteen years from now? Would she still be able to speak the language, would she still be mixing with Aborigines, would these moments be lost forever, or would they have played a big part in shaping her life, and her character. Looking at her laughing and talking with everyone, it was impossible to imagine it being any other way. Young Sophie had learnt about so many ways of the Yolngu that her life had already been blessed...Shirley had seen to that.

I went down to the lake with Shirley's brother, Harry, and found out about the legend of how this water came about.

In the Dreamtime, a snake bird, or a darter as it is called in Shirley's country, took off to where Lake Evella is now. Where it landed its wings touched the ground, and it formed a hole in the ground. Then it flew off toward Gapuwiyak again, and this time it landed in the middle of where the lake is now. It tried to fly away again but fresh water weeds started to come out of the ground, and took hold of the darter, and wouldn't let it take off again. As the bird was flapping its wings trying to get away, water started to come out of the ground and then Lake Evella was formed. The bird was trapped in the lake forever.

Not a sound and hardly a ripple. The burning off in the distance gave the sky an eerie glow. There was something really powerful about the moment. It was so serene, yet I felt there was something else. Harry told me that in certain areas around the lake tribal ceremonies and rituals were often held and a lot of these were off limits to most of the community. It sent a shiver right through me.

We walked back up the path to where everyone was sitting around in the shade of the mango tree. The original group of about five or six had now grown to about twelve or thirteen, and there were more coming in. Shirley introduced me to her family, and to some of the traditional owners of the land, as well as some of the other community members.

This was all a very rare honour for me. I sat there not wanting to move, not wanting to say anything at all. These people were sitting around swapping yarns, or just catching up with business in their own language. Even though some spoke different dia-lects, they could understand and contribute without any problems. I was just hoping that nobody would ask me something in boring old English, because that would have broken the magic. I wanted to stay where I was, and listen to this for hours and hours. Then it came home to me, I was now a guest in their country, and the language I spoke from my world was a second or third language up here in east Arnhem Land.

Shirley Nirrpurranydji was well respected alright! All of these people, including tribal leaders of the community, had come to visit and pay their respects. As I walked away, I looked back at the people under the tree. I had known Shirley for only a few hours, but it was enough to realise how much of an impression she has made on this place.

Through the night I heard clap sticks and other music and chanting. The following day someone told me what it was all about. It was part of the circumcision ceremony for the young boys at Gapuwiyak. This would go on for about two weeks, to get them ready for the big day. Things were happening all around me all the time.

The Gapuwiyak Community School is a non-bilingual school, which means the children are taught in straight English, and their own language is spoken at home and elsewhere. This decision to teach in English was made by the people themselves, in a clear message that they want their kids to be given access to the outside world. This hasn't always been the thinking in the past. Another change in education in this part of Australia is the program called Aboriginalisation. The Northern Territory education department and the commonwealth scheme is designed to promote Yolngu people into role model positions across the board in many areas, specifically for the children, so they can see their own kind achieving goals. Education for the Aborigine, by the Aborigine, is the aim of the experts. Hopefully it will encourage and influence these children. Shirley (who in 1993 became school principal) is the role model they look up to at Lake Evella. She has good "two-way learning". The worst thing you could ever do with this vibrant woman is under-estimate her. Don't be fooled by the surroundings or the lifestyle. She has been deep into both cultures and knows them very well, having represented the Yolngu educators at department meetings in Darwin and nationally in Canberra.

The words keep ringing in her head...going around and around...Aboriginalisation! Aboriginalisation! But it is not that simple for her. "So far with this Aboriginalisation in the schooling system, different communities feel different to others, and even the people in some of those communities are sometimes divided. A lot of schools would like to see all Aboriginal teachers, teaching their own kids, but for me black and white should work together. I don't think it's bad...Balandas standing up in front of a class room teaching Aboriginal kids. Because sometimes, for example, I might not have enough English to express myself in a situation, whereas a Balanda has that. We can all help each other." She is seen as a bi-cultural leader in the community, because of her profession and her knowledge, balancing the two worlds as best she can.

I've got a telephone in the house, I've got television, I've got a table and chairs in the house, that doesn't mean I'm going to lose everything and become a Balanda.

Shirley understands non-Aboriginal culture, and describes it poetically: "Balandas come like a big strong wind that blows from one place to another, whereas for me, I stay here. This is my place, I won't take my feet somewhere else. That's how I see them, as a piece of paper blown by a strong wind, driven away, and landing somewhere else.

"I've got a telephone in the house, I've got television, I've got a table and chairs in the house, that doesn't mean I'm going to lose everything and become a Balanda. I am living in an Aboriginal community, and I call myself an Aborigine. I still eat damper, and I go hunting, and I cook everything under the ground. I am an Aboriginal person.

"I don't dance traditional dance here. I used to dance, but, I don't know. If there's a death on another community, we always come together and paint ourselves up, and somebody announces by singing. I always go and join in, but don't dance. I feel strongly that one of these days I've got to stand up and dance, and join in with my brothers and sisters.

"If I go to something where there's traditional singing going on, I often sit and listen to their music, and that music makes me cry, because there's people in my family that have gone and left. I always think of my old people who've gone away from this place. All the songs and the singing is something spiritual for me, and for everyone here, and we all join in. If one person cries then everyone cries. It's the extended family thing, it's close all the time."

If I, or some of the others, go to Darwin, everything is written in English, everything.

When I spoke to Shirley, she was looking forward to 1993 when she would become the principal of Gapuwiyak Community School. While she wrestles with the concept of Aboriginal-isation, the thought of teaching only in English broadens the smile a lot more: "It's so vital. If I, or some of the others, go to Darwin, everything is written in English, everything." She burns with a desire and conviction, for the teaching of the young ones, for all of us to help Aboriginal children get the chance at least.

"The young people of this community are the future leaders for these people here. On the education side of things, we just don't have enough facilities, especially looking at the post-primary students. I feel strongly about this! There must be something done about all the kids who are leaving school, and who've got no jobs around town to go to! That's a big problem. I don't want to see kids walk into a shop without knowing the value of the money, and say, if a kid took ten dollars to a shop and didn't know what the change was! That's really my big worry for these children."

Today one person from Gapuwiyak attends an interstate college, and a handful are studying at Batchelor Teachers College outside Darwin.

All of this isn't enough. Shirley wants more of the children to

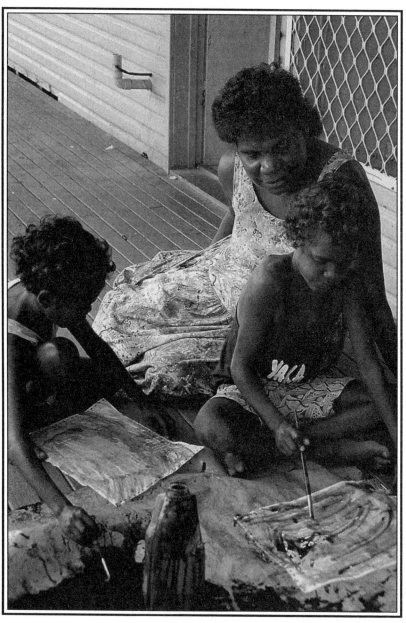

Shirley Nirrpurranydji with some of the students at Gapuwiyak school in Arnhem Land

turn up for class each day. On average one hundred and forty turn up each morning, out of the two hundred plus enrolled. Somehow she has to encourage the parents, inflate their self-pride and interest in their children's education.

The outside world is brought to the community through television and radio. Just as I saw their world, as a young boy, only as an image on the screen, they see the rest of Australia in exactly the same way. Shirley is helping to change that. She takes groups on a cultural and social exchange to Melbourne and Cairns, to expose them to the things they read about, and see on television, like the traffic in a big city, the lights, the millions of people, and all the noise. The last trip, Shirley had to help one or two of the kids going up the escalator, because their knees were trembling so much.

Shirley hopes her own children will at least make it to high school, something she never did. Her fifteen-year-old son is enquiring about the possibilities of boarding school, and that delights her very much.

In this vast land, buried away in a place most Australians will never see, is a woman who's lived a great deal, and has an enormous amount of living still to do. She is hidden away, but her role should not be dismissed as inconsequential.

Shirley grew up on nearby Elcho Island, with her mother and her mother's promised tribal husband. It was a small community heavily influenced by the missionaries, like so much else in northern Australia back then. Shirley went to the mission school on Elcho Island where she did very well with her studies. Making the junior choir was the start. That's when she really began to learn about the English language through a tour to Perth, community activities such as Christmas plays on the island, and a year at Kormilda Boarding College in Darwin.

It was a time of so many discoveries for Shirley. The world was opening up to this teenager. Finally in the early 1970s when she was seventeen, she put together some of the lost pieces of her family. She met her father and her new brothers and sisters for the first time. Now there was another new language to learn, at Gapuwiyak, where her father was a respected elder. He had helped build the airstrip and the roads. For the time being

Shirley's education was forgotten. Besides, her home was now Gapuwiyak, and there were other things to occupy her...namely her new found family, and the start of her own with her husband Wirrikuwuy. Shirley gave birth to a beautiful baby daughter in 1972, and presumably her life was mapped out, set to follow in the footsteps of the many Yolngu women before her. But she couldn't shake it that easily! There was work in a shop at the community, then she was approached by the school to help out as an assistant teacher.

> **I thought I didn't have enough English and enough brains to succeed.**

From a moment somewhere back in that time, Shirley made the commitment to stay with it, from then on. "After a few years at the school, I made up my mind to at least give the Aboriginal Teacher Education Centre at Batchelor a go. I'd thought about it for a while, then in 1979 I did my first year, and passed alright. Now that was a big surprise, because I thought I didn't have enough English and enough brains to get into the institution and succeed. That was a really difficult first year, because I had my third child to worry about, as well as my other kids, and the pressure was there. I did feel like coming back to the community for good and waiting until the children were all grown up, and then finishing my studies." Shirley did go back to Gapuwiyak, and stayed for a few years, to be with the new addition to her family, and in 1982 returned to college and passed her second year, followed by another successful campaign in 1983, her third and final year. On the one hand there was her family to be cared for and nurtured, while on the other she was juggling exams and the pressures of her own ambitions.

Plenty of perseverance and courage had carried her through. Against at times insurmountable odds, including a fair portion of self-doubt, Shirley now stood proud. "I had achieved my goal of becoming a teacher, not simply an assistant teacher. I went back to Gapuwiyak and worked for the next four years with my people. But I wanted to go even further. In 1988 I did my fourth year at Batchelor College, on a special program with Deakin University which offers Aborigines the qualifications to teach at any school, black or white. This was something very special. I graduated with a Bachelor of Arts in education. Sometimes I wonder how I got through, because it was so difficult to go back to studies. I must've tried very hard."

Over the years Shirley has accumulated all the necessary know-how, including an enjoyable term at a school at Nhulunbuy on the coast of Arnhem Land with about seven hundred children, including about twenty Aborigines. Another community, another lifestyle with a different emphasis for those Aboriginal children. Nevertheless an experience Shirley was grateful for, and one of the many that opened up her mind just a fraction more.

I see myself now as a strong person. I can stand up and talk for myself! In Aboriginal society, women are seen as weak. My brothers culturally are much stronger.

The Yolngu people in Gapuwiyak realise they have a special one amongst them, and for that, she is well respected and admired. Firstly in the traditional way, because her father is one of the head men of the tribe, and secondly for what she's earned herself, as a teacher, and a leader. "A lot of people say to me, you're a strong woman. I see myself now as a strong person. I can stand up and talk for myself! No matter what men say to me, I've got every right to say anything. In our society, women are seen as weak. Here in Arnhem Land, Aboriginal women in tribal clan groups traditionally aren't seen as being as strong as the men. A father will pass on all the traditional and ceremonial secrets to his sons and not to his daughters. My brothers culturally are much stronger, and will take over the family when my father passes away. But with my work, I'm seen as somebody who's here to help the others in the community."

Walking around with her, or just sitting back and watching, there was no question about that at all. Shirley Nirrpurranydji was a busy lady, very much in demand. Apart from holding her own family together, and being its guiding light, there was her work with the church, her work of course at school, and nowadays she was even called out to work her magic as a social worker — strictly as a friend — but she had been asked to intervene in family matters in the community on more than one occasion. Undoubtedly a flattering pat on the back but also an extra burden Shirley found hard to cope with sometimes.

Thanks to Shirley and some of the other women, Gapuwiyak is a "dry" community. Alcohol was crippling her people; she couldn't stand by and watch. A car accident and the suicide death of a young man in the community, were the breaking points for Shirley and her friends. She grabbed a megaphone and a few mates, and took to the streets, walking around speaking to the people, protesting about the destruction of their whole lifestyle. Despite what the men whispered in the back rooms, the women wanted to show their concern. Support came from others, including a few of the men. The community decided to ban alcohol from Lake Evella, and heavily fine offenders.

"Big difference now. Everybody's just wanting to go out bush, and live out bush, and not to worry about alcohol in this community. Just go our way with our own family, and that's it! Forget about this problem with ŋanitji."

For myself I reckon it's the colours of Arnhem Land that make it magical. Or maybe it's the light! You'll have to get up there and check it out for yourself. For some reason the light is different. It's like a diffuser has been put across the sky to make everything a little softer. It's strange, but it really made me feel good.